"Augustine of Hippo remains one of the towering figures in the history of the church. In this learned mini-treatise, Ian Clary takes us on a journey around some of the lesser-known foothills of the African bishop's theology of grace. I am happy to commend this study in theologically-driven pastoral care that feeds both mind and soul."

Lee Gatiss, PhD, Cambridge University, Director of Church Society and Adjunct Lecturer in Church History at Union School of Theology, Wales

"In my view, the best theologians God has given to the church are pastor-theologians. John Calvin, John Owen, Jonathan Edwards, and on. But standing above the aforementioned is Augustine, the greatest pastor-theologian to date. This small book by one of Canada's most promising up-and-coming Christian scholars will prove an accessible but also historically reliable look at Augustine's pastoral theology and his role in the later Pelagian controversy. Not essential reading, but certainly enjoyable reading!"

Mark Jones, PhD, Leiden University, Pastor of Faith Presbyterian Church in Vancouver, British Columbia, Research Associate at the University of the Free State (Bloemfontein)

"One of the challenges each pastor faces is faithfully to explain the biblical tensions between divine sovereignty and human responsibility. By his analysis of two of the lesser known writings of Augustine on the subject of grace and free will, Ian Clary has provided the modern-day pastor-theologian with a model of using theology in service of the church."

G. Stephen Weaver Jr., PhD, Southern Baptist Theological Seminary, Senior Pastor, Farmdale Baptist Church in Frankfort, Kentucky

"The influence of Augustine of Hippo towers above others in the history of the church, and yet our familiarity with him today is comparatively very slight—and this is especially the case with regard to Augustine as a *pastor*-theologian and his later role in the controversies with the "semi-Pelagians." It is here that Ian Clary's introductory work makes a helpful contribution. Good history and good theology carefully stated and clearly presented."

Fred G. Zaspel, PhD, Free University of Amsterdam, Pastor of Reformed Baptist Church of Franconia, Pennsylvania, Professor of Theology at Calvary Baptist Seminary

God Crowns His Own Gifts

GOD CROWNS HIS OWN GIFTS

Augustine, Grace, and the Monks of Hadrumetum

IAN HUGH CLARY

Copyright © Ian Hugh Clary 2021

H&E Academic, Peterborough, Ontario
www.hesedandemet.com

All rights reserved. This book may not be reproduced, in whole or in part, without written permission from the publishers.

Cover design by Chance Faulkner
Cover image drawing by Marcos Rodrigues
Image colourization by Paul Cox, www.reftoons.com

Paperback ISBN: 978-1-77484-019-1
Hardcover ISBN: 978-1-77484-021-4
Ebook ISBN: 978-1-77484-020-7

To:
John and Jillian Bell
Justin and Elisha Galotti
Clint and Christel Humfrey

For your "harmoniousness and trusty friendship"
(Augustine's words for his friend Alypius)

"The fear of God with rigid rules restrains,
But love with confidence throws down the reins."

John Searle, based on
his reading of Augustine's Letter CXLIV.3

Contents

Foreword xiii
   David Robinson

Preface xvii

Augustine and the Pastor-Theologians 1

1. Augustine's Two Letters 5

2. "The Grace of God Conquered":
Predestination, Polemics, and Penmanship 9

3. "The Gratuitousness of Grace":
The Theology of *Epistula* 194 21

4. "The Grace of God With Him":
The Theology of *De gratia et libero arbitrio* 37

5. Augustine the Pastor-Theologian 51

6. Augustine Matters Today 91

Works Cited 95

Subject Index 105

Scripture Index 109

Foreword

I insist that my students read primary sources and I often use Augustine to illustrate my point: "Don't just read books about Augustine," I say, "read Augustine." The corpus of Augustine's work is so huge that very few people can honestly claim to have read it all. Long ago, Isadore of Seville (*c.*560–636) said that anyone claiming to have read all of Augustine's writings is a liar. We should not be intimidated, however. Ian Clary's little book reminds us that we have much to learn, even from studying a small sample of his writing.

Augustine was arguably the greatest mind of his generation, but I admire him because he also had a big heart. As Clary demonstrates in the following pages, Augustine was a theologian and a pastor. Many of his writings are controversial. He wrote against the Manicheans, the Arians, the Pagans, the Donatists, and the Pelagians. We can read these writings superficially and charge him with being partisan and polemical. I remember reading a short article about Augustine in *The Economist* a few years ago entitled "Warrior of the Word." It characterized Augustine as a tyrant bishop who

Foreword

insisted he was right and everyone else was wrong. Yes, he had his weaknesses and his blind spots (e.g., sexuality); however, he saw himself as a *servus Verbi*, a servant of the Word, who was called to impart God's Word to those entrusted to his pastoral care.

One of my favourite passages in the *Confessions* (VII.ix.13–14) is where Augustine remembers reading the books of the Platonists. He read there that the Logos was eternal, but those books said nothing about the Word becoming flesh and dwelling among us (John 1:14). Those books did not say anything about the Word taking on the form of a servant and humbling himself in obedience to point of death on a cross (Philippians 2:6–11). Augustine became a disciple of the One who calls us and says, "learn from me, for I am gentle and lowly in heart, and you will find rest for your souls" (Matthew 11:28). He was not a "warrior of the Word." He was a servant of the Word. We call him *doctor gratiae*, the teacher of grace, but he was also *servus gratiae*, the servant or minister of grace. Ian Clary helps us see both sides of Augustine. Yes, Augustine is big and few of us will ever read or fully appreciate everything he wrote. Clary has not tried for a comprehensive account. He has selected and analyzed two writings, so that we might see Augustine from two different perspectives, as a pastor and as a theologian. To be a servant

GOD CROWNS HIS OWN GIFTS

of the Word and a servant of grace, we need to have a sharp mind and a soft heart. Clary shows us that Augustine had both and, thus, he is a model for Christian leaders today.

David Robinson, PhD
Pastor, Westminster Chapel, Toronto, ON
Lecturer in Church History, Tyndale University College

Preface

The original manuscript for this book was written and defended as a master of divinity thesis completed at The Toronto Baptist Seminary and Bible College in 2008; it has since undergone extensive revision. At the time I completed the thesis I felt a sense of loss that my "time with Augustine" had come to a close, so I am thankful for the chance to return to him for this latest incarnation of a manuscript that has gone through many forms.

Why visit and revisit Augustine? The obvious answer is that Augustine's impact not only on the church but Western thought as a whole since the fifth century is incalculable. I am shaped by his work in ways that I cannot begin to fathom. As a result, secondary works on his theology and philosophy have developed into a veritable cottage industry. In spite of this flood the book you are holding in your hand does fill a lacuna as it focuses on two areas of relative neglect in Augustinian studies: his role in the later Pelagian controversy, and his pastoral theology. This why it I consider it a special privilege to delve into both of these matters.

Preface

Thanks are due my supervisor, Michael A.G. Haykin, for introducing me to the field of ancient Christian studies and for helping me tread the monstrous deep of Augustinian studies. My examiners J. Stephen Yuille and Kirk Wellum are to be thanked for advice on improving the original; Dr. Yuille especially for his suggestion of Harry J. McSorley's section on Augustine and the will in *Luther: Right or Wrong?*

I am also thankful for my colleagues in the School of Theology at Colorado Christian University, namely my dean, Dr. David Kotter, as well as Megan DeVore (an expert in the ancient Church), John Wind, Michael Plato, Matt Jones, Kevin Turner, Seth Rodriguez, and David Bosworth. A huge thanks also to Elise Hegarty and her impeccable editorial skills. I am also thankful for the support of our president, Dr. Don Sweeting, a great lover of the Christian past and Augustine especially.

Thanks are also due to Drs. Michael Haykin, David Robinson and Heather Weir, and pastors Clint Humfrey and David Shedden, for giving an earlier draft the once over. I am also thankful to Dr. Robinson for the kind foreword—he is a dear friend and an excellent patristics scholar.

It has been great to work with my publisher H&E Publishing, and especially Chance Faulkner. I am very thankful for the work they are doing. I especially love the cover image of an older, obviously North African Augustine that was developed by Marcos Rodriques, and how the cover looks like an homage to the cover of Henry Chadwick's great biography of Augustine. Great work guys!"

To borrow a cliché: I take full responsibility for any insufficiencies of argument or style in this work.

Now that I am living and teaching in Colorado, my family and I have found a great church whose pastor embodies the ethos of Augustine as outlined in this book. I am very thankful to Ryan Wassell and Redeeming Grace Church of Lakewood, CO, for great friendship and fellowship.

As I wrote the latter part of this book, I became acutely aware of the influence of a number of men who, as with Augustine and the monks of Hadrumetum, mentored me. I am truly thankful for Drs. Michael Haykin and Dennis Ngien. God has used them in my life at various times to great benefit. A like encouragement has been from three dear friends and their wives, to whom I dedicate this book. These are John Bell and his wife Jillian (New City Baptist Church in Toronto, ON); Justin Galotti and his wife Elisha (West Toronto Baptist Church); and Clint Humfrey and his wife Christel (Calvary Grace Community Church in Calgary,

Preface

AB). These three ministers of the gospel stand in the Augustinian tradition and model what it means to be a pastor-theologian. With deep gratitude, I dedicate this book to them.

Final thanks are to my wife Vicky and our four children Jack, Molly, Kate, and Tom. May God crown his gifts in you.

Ian Clary
Lent 2020

Augustine and the Pastor-Theologians

Modern evangelicals have been guarded about the early church. Thankfully, as D.H. Williams observes, "Discussion of the place and value of the great tradition is taking place among pastors and laity in denominations that have normally regarded it as irrelevant or as a hindrance to authentic Christian belief and spirituality."[1] He wrote this fifteen years ago, and thankfully things have progressed since then, but there is still a lot of work to be done.[2] Williams believes that evangelicals are suspicious of the church fathers because they are the domain of Roman Catholicism. However, since the sixteenth century, the fathers have played an integral role in Protestant theology. Stephen R. Holmes says, "[T]he mainstream Reformation project sought to be responsible to the tradition as it had been passed down, even when disagreeing

---

[1] D. H. Williams, *Evangelicals and Tradition: The Formative Influence of the Early Church* (Grand Rapids: Baker Academic, 2005), 15.

[2] I am privileged to serve as a fellow of two institutions that are seeking to bring the riches of the Christian past to bear on evangelicals, namely the Andrew Fuller Center for Baptist Studies and the Center for Baptist Renewal.

sharply with certain aspects of it."[3] Today's Protestants should "rediscover" the fathers for use in the twenty-first century.[4]

In this age of theological fatuity, the early church seems drably involved in arid debates over abstract theology. With today's stress on praxis and the confused notion that "doctrine divides," the fathers seem out of touch with the realities of twenty-first century ministry. What is forgotten is that most of the key church fathers were pastors. Ignatius of Antioch (ca. 35–ca. 107), Polycarp of Smyrna (69–155), Athanasius of Alexandria (ca. 296–373), Basil of Caesarea (330–377/79), Gregory of Nazianzus (ca. 329–390) and Augustine of Hippo (354–430) were all bishops in the cities that qualify their names. Their theology was not leisurely penned in the comfort of ivory towers; rather, these leaders wrote under the threat of persecution—Ignatius and Polycarp were martyrs, Athanasius was exiled five times—as they sought to be faithful to the teaching of the church. There is no better image of what is today called the "pastor-theologian" than the picture of Athanasius sitting brazenly in his bishop's chair as

---

[3] Stephen R. Holmes, *Listening to the Past: The Place of Tradition in Theology* (Grand Rapids: Baker Academic, 2002), 2.

[4] A good start would be Michael A. G. Haykin, *Rediscovering the Church Fathers: Who They Were and How They Shaped the Church* (Wheaton: Crossway Books, 2011).

his congregants fled a hostile Arian mob who beat down the cathedral door in Alexandria.[5] They wanted to kill him because he held to orthodox Christology.

A preeminent example of a pastor-theologian from early church history is Augustine whose impact on history cannot be overstated; his influence reaches beyond the Catholic-Protestant divide into western intellectual history as a whole. As Carol Harrison says, Augustine "stands at a watershed in the history of western thought, between the classical world of the Roman empire and the Middle Ages."[6] Known as *doctor gratiae*, Augustine's marriage of grace and free will dominates discussions of the subject from the medieval scholastics through the Reformation to today. His concern for theological acuity and pastoral sensitivity in the Pelagian contro-

---

[5] John Piper, *Contending for Our All: Defending Truth and Treasuring Christ in the Lives of Athanasius, John Owen and, J. Gresham Machen* (Wheaton: Crossway, 2006), 54. The term "pastor-theologian" has become a vogue way of describing the pastor who is theologically-minded; cf. Owen Strachan, "The (Welcome) Rise of the Pastor-Theologian: A Friendly response to Donald Miller," http://thegospelcoalition.org/blogs/tgc/2011/04/26/the-welcome-rise-of-the-pastor-theologian-a-friendly-response-to-donald-miller/ (accessed August 27, 2011); Paul Brewster, *Andrew Fuller: Model Pastor-Theologian* Baptist Thought and Life (Nashville: B&H Academic, 2010).

[6] Carol Harrison, "Augustine (353–430)" in Adrian Hastings, Alistair Mason and Hugh Pyper eds., *Key Thinkers in Christianity* (Oxford: Oxford University Press, 2003), 24.

versy over grace and free will shows Augustine as an exemplary pastor and theologian. Due to his influence, it should come as no surprise that much has been written on his doctrine of grace. This book focuses on an area of Augustinian historiography that has escaped the historical-theologian's eye by comparing two of his lesser-studied writings on the relationship between grace and free will. This comparison sheds light not only on the theology of the later Augustine, but also his character as a pastor-theologian.

1

Augustine's Two Letters

Admittedly it is not unique to write on grace and free will in Augustine's general theology.[1] Less attention, however, has been paid to his role in the so-called "semi-Pelagian" controversy; relatively few scholars have studied the broader issues involved in the four treatises called *Answer to the Pelagians IV*.[2] In this book, I assess two documents: Augustine's

---

[1] See, for instance, the bibliography at the end of Marianne Djuth, "Liberty" in Allan D. Fitzgerald ed., *Augustine Through the Ages: An Encyclopedia* (Grand Rapids/Cambridge: William B. Eerdmans, 1999), 497–498.

[2] St. Augustine, *Answer to the Pelagians, IV: To the Monks of Hadrumetum and Provence* in Roland J. Teske trans. *The Works of Saint Augustine: A Translation for the 21st Century* 1.26 (Hyde Park: New City Press, 1999). For the sake of this study the terms "monks of Hadrumetum" will be used instead of semi-Pelagian. For more on why the term semi-Pelagian is not helpful see Mary Alphonsine Lesousky, *The De Dono Perseverantiae of Saint Augustine: A Translation with An Introduction and Commentary* (Washington: The Catholic University of America Press, 1956), 35–39; Roland J. Teske, "General Introduction" in Roland J. Teske trans. *Answer to the Pelagians, IV: To the Monks of Hadrumetum and Provence* in *The Works of Saint Augustine: A Translation for the 21st Century* 1.26 (Hyde Park: New City Press, 1999), 11; Conrad Leyser, "Semi-Pelagianism" in Allan D. Fitzgerald ed., *Augustine Through the Ages: An Encyclopedia* (Grand Rapids/Cambridge: William B. Eerdmans, 1999), 761–766. See especially Donato Ogliari, *Gratia et Certamen: The Relationship Between Grace and Free Will in the Discussion of Augustine with the So-Called Semipelagians* (Leuven, Belgium: Leuven University Press, 2003), 5–9.

letter to Sixtus (*Epistula* 194) and his treatise *De gratia et libero arbitrio*.³ Augustine wrote the former to a priest in Rome to squash any Pelagian sympathies. Rebecca Harden Weaver explains that in the letter Augustine argued for the "utterly gratuitous character of grace" against the Pelagians, whose teaching over-emphasized the freedom of the human will.⁴ The latter was written to reassure some confused North African monks in the theological backwater of Hadrumetum that God's invincible grace does not destroy free choice. Of this Donato Ogliari says, "[T]he bishop of Hippo could now pay greater attention to resisting the denial of the existence of free will."⁵

In scholarly discussion concerning the events of the monastery in Hadrumetum the relationship between *Epistula* 194

---

³ Augustine, "Epistle 194" in *Saint Augustine: Letters Volume IV (165-203)* trans. Wilfrid Parsons (New York: Fathers of the Church, Inc., 1955), 301-332; Augustine, "Grace and Free Choice" in Roland J. Teske trans., *Answer to the Pelagians, IV: To the Monks of Hadrumetum and Provence*. In *The Works of Saint Augustine: A Translation for the 21ˢᵗ Century* 1.26 (Hyde Park: New City Press, 1999), 71-106.

⁴ Rebecca Harden Weaver, *Divine Grace and Human Agency: A Study of the Semi-Pelagian Controversy* (Macon: Mercer University Press, 1996), 5. For Pelagianism see Peter Brown, "Pelagius and His Supporters: Aims and Environment," *Journal of Theological Studies* XIX.1 (April 1968): 93-114. See also Eugene TeSelle, "Pelagius, Pelagianism" in Allan D. Fitzgerald ed., *Augustine Through the Ages: An Encyclopedia* (Grand Rapids/Cambridge: William B. Eerdmans, 1999), 633-640.

⁵ Ogliari, *Gratia et Certamen*, 58.

and *De gratia et libero arbitrio* is only casually referred to. It is said that Augustine is attentive to the character of grace when writing to Sixtus and pays more attention to free will in the treatise to Hadrumetum. Weaver argues,

> In this letter [to Sixtus] the bishop of Hippo had stressed his views regarding human nature and divine grace. He had insisted that the human condition as fallen in Adam is incapable of attaining merit on its own. Furthermore, he had argued that grace is utterly gratuitous; it is given totally apart from any human deserving to those whom it chooses. Somewhat in contrast to his position in this letter is the argument that he made in *De gratia et libero arbitrio*. In this treatise... Augustine tried to maintain the reality of the human free will, and he insisted that divine reward is given to human merit.[6]

Ogliari concurs: "It is true that in the *De gratia et libero arbitrio* there is a kind of 'front reversal' with regard to the way Augustine approached the problem of nature and grace during the Pelagian controversy."[7] Unfortunately no further development of this "front reversal" is offered. This study, then, explores the claim that there is a difference in emphasis over grace and free will between the two

---

[6] Weaver, *Divine Grace and Human Agency*, 4.
[7] Ogliari, *Gratia et Certamen*, 58.

documents and accounts for this difference theologically and pastorally.

In the first part of this book our thoughts are directed to Augustine's teaching on grace and free will in his broader work, with focus on *Epistula* 194 and *De gratia et libero arbitrio*. In this section I give attention to topics like sin, human ability and merit, responsibility and sovereignty, and future rewards. The purpose of this first section is to highlight the emphases of grace or free will in each of the documents evaluated to justify and give clarity to what Weaver and Ogliari contend. The second section accounts for the difference in emphasis by evaluating historical background and authorial intent—theology should never be done in an historical vacuum, and it is of great help to determine meaning by examining historical context. In the case of these two letters, Augustine proves himself to be an exemplar of pastoral care; both as a defender and teacher of the people of God. As for pastoral theology, Augustine's letters to the troubled monks are of great value to the church as they serve as models of theologically-driven pastoral care.

2

"The Grace of God Conquered": Predestination, Polemics, and Penmanship

Doctor gratiae

The question of the relationship between divine sovereignty and human responsibility is frequently addressed by Augustine from his earliest writings, though experts are divided on the nature and development of this relationship. John M. Rist notes a lack of consensus among scholars and says that the subsequent "struggle to determine Augustine's view of free will and grace has continued with unabated vigour and often unabated ferocity."[1] In what follows, I offer a brief overview of Augustine's writings on grace and free will, with definition of terms.

---

[1] John M. Rist, "Augustine on Free Will and Predestination," *Journal of Theological Studies* 20.2 (1969): 421. Cf. Eleonore Stump, "Augustine on free will" in Eleonore Stump and Norman Kretzmann eds., *The Cambridge Companion to Augustine* (Cambridge: Cambridge University Press, 2004), 124, who agrees with Rist. Much of the problem has to do with the development of Augustine's theology as he matured.

Predestination, Polemics, and Penmanship

The first use of "will" (*voluntas*) occurs early on in Augustine's career, in the anti-Manichaean *De duabus animabus* 10.14 (392/393).[2] From this time on *voluntas* makes regular appearances up to his final *De dono perseverantiae* (428/429).[3] Between 387/388 and 395, the period spanned when he wrote *De libero arbitrio*, Augustine focused on the nature of the will with the hope of formulating an answer to the origin of evil, a subject written with an eye towards upsetting Manichaean dualism, arguing for what Simon Harrison describes as "a monist view of the universe: God is the one and only principle."[4] According to Augustine, God is not the author of moral evil; its first cause is human freedom. As Augustine says at the very beginning of Book One of his dialogue with his friend Evodius:[5]

---

[2] Marianne Djuth, "Will" in Allan D. Fitzgerald ed., *Augustine Through the Ages: An Encyclopedia* (Grand Rapids/Cambridge: Wm. B. Eerdmans, 1999), 883.

[3] Cf. Lesousky, *The De dono perseverantiae of Saint Augustine: A Translation with an Introduction and a Commentary* (Washington: Catholic University of America Press, 1956).

[4] Cf. Simon Harrison, *Augustine's Way Into the Will: The Theological and Philosophical Significance of* De libero arbitrio, Oxford Early Christian Studies (Oxford: Oxford University Press, 2006), 14–16. Harrison gives a convincing argument of the unity of *De libero arbitrio*.

[5] There is some debate as to whether Augustine originally wrote this as a dialogue with Evodius; his interlocutor's name first appears in manuscripts dating from the middle ages. See Harrison, *Augustine's Way Into the Will*, 2.

GOD CROWNS HIS OWN GIFTS

> Well, if you know or believe that God is good...then He does not *do* evil. On the other hand, if we grant that God is just ... then He rewards the good; by the same token, He hands out punishments to evildoers, punishments that are doubtless evils to those who suffer them. Accordingly, if no one pays penalties unjustly...then God is indeed the author of evils of type (*b*), though not in any way the author of evils of type (*a*).[6]

While the will is the dominant theme of *De libero arbitrio*, in the *defensio* of it in *Retractationes* 1.9.4 Augustine wryly observes that he was not exactly silent about divine grace either.

De libero arbitrio is the key transitional treatment of the freedom of the will in Augustine's work. It was initially written in the early days of Pelagianism and is not marked by any significant interaction with the heresy. However, *De libero arbitrio* is important for an understanding of Augustine on the will as he continued to work on it throughout his later career and as his later anti-Pelagian writings do not differ substantially from it.[7] Free will, Augustine says, is a gift from

---

[6] Augustine, *On the Free Choice of the Will, On Grace and Free Choice, and Other Writings* Cambridge Texts in the History of Philosophy, ed., Peter King (Cambridge: Cambridge University Press, 2010), 3.

[7] Harrison, *Augustine's Way Into the Will*, 27. See also Harry J. McSorley, *Luther: Right or Wrong?* (New York/Minneapolis: Newman Press/Augsburg Publishing, 1969), 66. Harrison notes a methodological difference between *De*

God, though it can be misused.[8] Sin—an absence of good—is an act of the will, and while God foreknows sin, he does not cause it.[9] For a person to be truly free, they must follow the law of God, though a person is only guilty of sin if they are obliged to do or not do something.[10]

As important as *De libero arbitrio* is to the Augustinian corpus, and as much as it possesses the florescence of his later thought, the relationship between grace and free will is not worked to the maturity of his later writing; this maturation comes in stages. *De diversis quaestionibus ad Simplicianum* (396/397), written to Ambrose's successor Simplician (d. ca. 400) in Milan, is the first stage; it is a gateway to Augustine's growing reflection on grace.[11] The letter is the earliest fledged statement on the subject and contains all the elements of his later anti-Pelagianism. In particular, Augustine

---

libero arbitrio and *De gratia et libero arbitrio*, as the latter is more reliant on Scripture texts than the former. This is so, says Harrison, because the earlier tract was concerned with contradicting the Manichees who were not familiar with biblical teaching (Harrison, *Augustine's Way Into the Will*, 27).

[8] *De libero arbitrio* 2.1.1-3.
[9] *De libero arbitrio* 1.1.1; 2.20.54 ; 3.2.4-3.
[10] *De libero arbitrio* 2.20.54; 3.16.45.
[11] Peter King's otherwise good introduction to a recent translation of Augustine's writings on grace and free will curiously does not mention the importance of *Ad Simplicianum* in Augustine's theological development. Peter King, "Introduction" in Augustine, *On the Free Choice of the Will, On Grace and Free Choice, and Other Writings* Cambridge Texts in the History of Philosophy, ed., Peter King (Cambridge: Cambridge University Press, 2010), ix-xxxiii.

speaks of election not as foreseeing, as he had previously,[12] but causative, grounded in the eternal decree.[13] He teaches that God is the primary mover in salvation who gives the sinner requisite faith.[14] Augustine also discusses the common themes of the hardening of Pharaoh and the *massa peccati*.[15] In *Retractationes* Augustine says that it was while writing *Ad Simplicianum* that his view on the necessity of grace changed:

> I, indeed, labored in defense of the free choice of the human will; but the grace of God conquered, and finally I was able to understand, with full clarity, the meaning of the Apostle: "For who singles thee out? Or what hast thou that thou has not received? And if thou

---

[12] See *Expositio quarundam propositionum ex epistula ad Romanos* 55; Book 3 of *De Libero Arbitrio*; Book 5 of *De civitate Dei*. Rist explains that "The two questions [foreknowledge and predestination] were originally distinct, coming from distinct historical worlds, and foreknowledge need not, of itself, entail predestination. However, when near the end of his life in 428/9, Augustine offers a definition of predestination, he claims that it is nothing other than God's 'foreknowledge and preparation of those acts of kindness (*beneficia*) by which those who are saved are saved' (*The Gift of Perseverance* 14.35)." John M. Rist, *Augustine: Ancient Thought Baptized* (Cambridge: Cambridge University Press, 1996), 269.

[13] *Ad Simplicianum* 1.2.6.
[14] *Ad Simplicianum* 1.2.9.
[15] *Ad Simplicianum* 1.2.15–16.

hast received it, why dost thou boast as if thou hadst not received it?"[16]

It is difficult to determine the way a fecund thinker like Augustine defines his terms—especially as it is common for scholars to think of the so-called earlier and later Augustine—so it is best to generally consider his theological vocabulary. As for his anti-Pelagianism, *voluntas* is the movement of "a rational soul without anyone compelling either for not losing or for acquiring something."[17] Rist says it is more than just a rational act: "*Voluntas* is not a decision-making faculty of the individual…but the individual himself. Hence it can be good or bad."[18] A person wills the good because he or she is good; likewise, a person wills evil because that person is evil. *Liberum arbitrium* is related to *voluntas*; Augustine maintains that everyone has freedom of choice, either for good or bad. Rist says,

> If we have formed good habits…then we shall make good choices freely … if, however, our habits are bad, then our choices in that area are bad. Yet although they

---

[16] *Retractationes* 2.1.1; cf. St. Augustine, *The Retractations* The Fathers of the Church trans., M. Inez Bogan (Washington: Catholic University of America Press, 1968), 120.

[17] Djuth, "Will," 883, this use is in reference to soteriology.

[18] Rist, "Augustine on Free Will and Predestination," 422.

are bad, they are still for Augustine free choices for which we are individually responsible.[19]

Not surprisingly, Augustine's first use of *praedestinavit* is in *Ad Simplicianum* (1.2.8), though Rist notes that it is only in verb form; the noun *praedestinatio* does not occur, as Augustine prefers *propositum* (plan).[20] Some scholars question whether Augustine holds to what is often called double-predestination, and if so, to what degree. There is evidence that he speaks of God predestining some to perdition—*Enchiridion* 26 (421/422) is suggestive: "Thence, after his [Adam's] sin, he was driven into exile, and by his sin the whole race of which he was the root was corrupted in him, and thereby subjected to the penalty of death."[21] As the "Supreme Good," God makes use of evil deeds for the damnation of those whom he had justly "predestined to punishment" and the salvation of those he had mercifully "predestined to grace."[22] However, Augustine's view of *massa peccati* (see below) and God's passing over of those left in sin indicates a more passive role of God in hardening—allowing sinners to

---

[19] Rist, "Augustine on Free Will and Predestination," 422.

[20] Rist, *Augustine*, 269.

[21] Augustine, *The Enchiridion on Faith, Hope and Love* (Washington: Regnery Publishing, 1996), 32.

[22] Rist, *Augustine*, 269. Rist also references *Epistula* 204.2 to Dulcitius and *De Anima et eius Origine* where the language of predestination to death is used.

harden themselves—than strong double-predestination language implies. In *De praedestinatione sanctorum* 17.34 (428/429) predestination is pretemporal, echoing Ephesians 1:4 as "before the establishment of the world." It allows for the free choice of the sinner who could reject the salvation offer and ultimately wind up in perdition. As Rist explains: "A possibility Augustine certainly ruled out is that God intended some (or all) of these to be saved, but was thwarted in that intention by man's sin."[23] God's plan was always to save some and allow others to proceed volitionally to their own demise. Why this is the case, and not a seemingly more compassionate universalism, Augustine says that God is most glorified in the expression of both his justice in damnation and mercy in salvation. The question, "Why does God not save everyone?" is not the one to ask, rather, "Why does God save anyone?"[24] John Searle well-captures Augustine's predestinarianism in verse: "Not only downwards drags the weight,/The Will that holds each thing in thrall;/Each finds its own determined state,/The flame must rise, the stone must fall."[25]

---

[23] Rist, *Augustine*, 270.

[24] Rist, *Augustine*, 273.

[25] Thankfully the poem—based on *Confessiones* 13.9—does not end here: "And I where'er I live and move/Must rise to Thee—my weight is love." John

GOD CROWNS HIS OWN GIFTS

Regarding the related term *gratia*, Gerald Bonner says, "It is unwise to seek to limit the operations of God's grace to [Augustine's] dogmatic formulations" because he is a "teacher of spirituality." As such, Augustine takes for granted "a desire for God naturally existing in the human soul by reason of its creation in *the image and likeness of God*."[26] This desire not withstanding, because of their sin condition inherited from Adam, humans need divine power to do the good; they need grace. *Gratia* in the writings of Augustine, as Peter King observes, is "supererogatory" on the part of God.[27] Saving grace is "the ultimate benefit God can confer" and is conferred antecedent to human merit.[28] It is "that divine operation in angels and humans through which they are moved to know and love God"—it is the illumination of the mind by divine Truth, the Word of God, and the

---

Searle, *Verses from St. Augustine, or Specimens from a Rich Mine* (Oxford: Oxford University Press, 1953), 28.

[26] Gerald Bonner, *Freedom and Necessity: St. Augustine's Teaching on Divine Power and Human Freedom* (Washington: The Catholic University of America Press, 2007), 59.

[27] King, "Introduction," xxv. King sees a four-fold use of grace in Augustine's writings: G1 – salvation; G2 – good works; G3 – perseverance; G4 – *initium fidei* (beginning of faith).

[28] King, "Introduction," xxv.

movement of the will by divine Love, the Holy Spirit.[29] In *De spiritu et littera* (412), Augustine identifies grace with the Holy Spirit, who is given by God to draw sinners to faith and repentance.[30] In *Retractationes* 1.9, defending his use of terms in *De libero arbitrio*, Augustine says that any good in the human will is a gift of God. Grace does not merely assist the will but controls it "since if there is any point at which the will is unassisted in welcoming assistance, the final end is cast into doubt."[31]

It would appear from these definitions that grace and free will are incompatible; however, such is not the case. Augustine often presupposes the reality of both grace and free will and speaks of them in the same context. What he does not do is reconcile them ultimately. In the words of Gotthard Nygren, "The impression cannot be avoided that here there is a clear paradox. This paradoxical character is henceforth inseparably connected with Augustine's theology."[32] While

---

[29] J. Patout Burns, "Grace" in Allan D. Fitzgerald ed., *Augustine Through the Ages: An Encyclopedia* (Grand Rapids/Cambridge: Wm. B. Eerdmans, 1999), 391, 398.

[30] *De spiritu et littera* 3.5; 5.7.

[31] Henry Chadwick, *Augustine of Hippo: A Life* (Oxford: Oxford University Press, 2009), 152.

[32] Gotthard Nygren, *Das Pradestinationsproblem in der Theologie Augustins* Forschungen zur Kirchen und Dogmengeschichte 5 (Göttingen: Vandenhoeck and Ruprecht, 1956), 47, cited in McSorley, *Luther*, 76.

GOD CROWNS HIS OWN GIFTS

the paradox is real on the part of the finite interpreter, its solution is clear in the mind of God.

With this brief understanding of grace and free choice in Augustine, it must be asked: What of their relationship in *Epistula* 194 and *De gratia et libero arbitrio*?

3

"The Gratuitousness of Grace": The Theology of *Epistula* 194

Of *Epistula* 194, written to Sixtus in the midst of the Pelagian controversy, B.B. Warfield says, "The greater part of [the letter] is given to a discussion of the gratuitousness of grace, which, just because grace, is given to no preceding merits."[1] The following is a survey of the contents of the letter as it pertains to this gratuitous grace.

Augustine delves into an explanation of grace early on in the letter. He starts by outlining the nature of the Pelagian complaint,

> When they think they are being deprived of their free will if they admit that man has no good will of his own without the help of God, they do not understand that they are not thus strengthening human free will but puffing it up so that it is carried off into empty space,

---

[1] B.B. Warfield, "Introductory Essay" in Philip Schaff ed., *Nicene and Post-Nicene Fathers Volume 5: Augustin: Anti-Pelagian Writings First Series* (Peabody: Hendrickson Publishers, 2004), xlix.

not anchored on the Lord as an immovable rock, for "the will is made ready by the Lord."[2]

This is, for Augustine, the crux of the Pelagian grievance. Their emphasis on the freedom of the human will, independent of the grace of God, leaves it ungrounded and arbitrary. However, for Augustine, grace is given freely and not based on merit. As Weaver says, "Any connection between the divine conferral of grace and human distinctions in merit would have the effect of making the former dependent on the latter. Grace would be a reward."[3] Mary Alphonsine Lesousky elaborates: "What merit does man have before grace, then, since there is no merit in us without grace, and when God crowns our merits, does He crown anything other than His own gifts?"[4] This last statement, borrowed from Augustine, "was the firebrand that set off the conflagration that was to become Semipelagianism," which is explored below.[5] The argument against the Pelagians, then, is "that free will is not nullified by the help of God. On the contrary...[it

---

[2] Augustine, "Epistle 194," 303.

[3] Rebecca Harden Weaver, *Divine Grace and Human Agency: A Study of the Semi-Pelagian Controversy* (Macon, Georgia: Mercer University Press, 1996), 5.

[4] Mary Alphonsine Lesousky, *The De Dono Perseverantiae of Saint Augustine: A Translation with An Introduction and Commentary* (Washington, D.C.: The Catholic University of America Press, 1956), 41.

[5] Lesousky, *The De dono perseverantiae of Saint Augustine*, 41 n.17.

is] made possible and sustained by his grace, on which [it is] firmly anchored as on a solid rock."[6]

Augustine appeals early in the letter to Proverbs 8:35 — "For my outgoings are the outgoings of life, and in them is prepared favour from the Lord" (LXX; ἑτοιμάζεται θέλησις παρὰ Κυρίου)—to demonstrate the need for setting a foundation for the will. Without such grounding in God, the will (θέλησις) is "condemned to float among vanities (*per inania feratur*)."[7]

Augustine regularly referred to the *massa damnata* or the *massa peccati* in his writings to indicate the lump of damnation or sin that all of Adam's progeny find themselves in.[8] In *Sermon* 26 he says, "Two little children are born. If you ask what is due, they both cleave to the lump of perdition. But why does its mother carry the one to grace, while the other is suffocated by its mother in her sleep? Both have deserved nothing of good, but the potter has power over the clay, of the same lump to make one vessel unto honor and another to

---

[6] Donato Ogliari, *Gratia et Certamen: The Relationship Between Grace and Free Will in the Discussion of Augustine with the So-Called Semipelagians* (Leuven, Belgium: Leuven University Press, 2003), 30–31.

[7] Ogliari, *Gratia et Certamen*, 31.

[8] Rist, quoting O. Rottmanner, summarizes Augustine's language: "[W]e are a *massa luti, peccati, peccatorum, iniquitatis, irae, mortis, perditionis, damnationis, offensionis, originis, vitiatae atque damnatae*; we are a *massa tota vitiata, damnabilis, damnata*." Quoted in Rist, "Augustine on Free Will and Predestination," 431. We saw above that he used it as early as *Ad Simplicianum*.

The Theology of *Epistula* 194

dishonor."[9] The concept of *massa damnata*, derived from Paul, explains the lot of humankind outside of grace. In *Epistula* 194 Augustine uses Romans 9 to show that God is not a respecter of persons,

> Where one and the same clay of damnation and offense is involved, there can be no respect had of persons, so that the saved may learn from the lost that the same punishment would have been his lot, also, if grace had not rescued him.[10]

Augustine sums his argument with a word about the relation of grace to merit: "If it is grace, it is obviously not awarded for any merit, but bestowed as a pure act of bounty."[11] This is followed by proof-texts from Romans 9–11 and an explanation of the nature of vessels of mercy and vessels of wrath.[12]

---

[9] Augustine, "Sermon 26" quoted in Gerald Bonner, *Freedom and Necessity: St. Augustine's Teaching on Divine Power and Human Freedom* (Washington, D.C.: The Catholic University of America Press, 2007), 24.

[10] Augustine, "Epistle 194," 303.

[11] Augustine, "Epistle 194," 303.

[12] Bonner says, "Such language, which is constantly repeated in Augustine's later writings, has persuaded many students that he ended his life as a complete supralapsarian predestinarian theologian, a hypercalvinist before Calvin was born." Bonner, *Freedom and Necessity*, 24.

GOD CROWNS HIS OWN GIFTS

The Pelagians vaingloriously believe that their merits precede God's action.[13] However, Augustine shows that even Pelagius, when seeking to dodge excommunication in Palestine, "anathematized" those who argue that the grace of God is given according to merit. Instead, there is only the belief that "merit regulates grace."[14] Augustine argues, contrarily, that grace justifies the wicked without regard to merit: "Therefore, the reception of this grace is not preceded by any merits because the wicked deserve punishment, not grace, and it would not be grace if it were awarded as something due and not freely given."[15] Later he avers, "But when we seek to know how mercy is deserved we find no merit because there is none, lest grace be made void if it is not freely given but awarded to merit."[16] As Lesousky summarizes, "Grace is given not because of the merits of any preceding will. Grace would not be grace if it were not given gratuitously."[17] According to Weaver, "The effect is that there is no correlation between God's generosity and any

---

[13] Augustine, "Epistle 194," 305.
[14] Augustine, "Epistle 194," 305–306.
[15] Augustine, "Epistle 194," 306.
[16] Augustine, "Epistle 194," 310.
[17] Lesousky, *The De dono perseverantiae of Saint Augustine*, 40.

pattern of human life. In fact, the relation of grace to meritorious life became the focus of Augustine's argument."[18]

God is not unjust by giving grace to some and leaving others to languish in the mass of perdition; Romans 9:18–20 says that God hardens whom he will because of his right as Potter over the clay. Augustine explains that "this hardening was deserved, and we find it to be so because the whole clay of sin was damned."[19] God's hardening is predicated by the reality that those hardened were already a part of the clay of sin. The role of God in hardening does not mean that he actively hardens a sinner; rather hardening is passive as God leaves the sinner to his or her own sin. "God does not harden by imparting malice to it [the clay of sin], but by not imparting mercy" to the sinner.[20] Moreover, due to the passive nature of God's hardening, he is free of the charge of injustice. Divine justice accomplishes what is deserved by sinful men.[21] In *Ad Simplicianum*, Augustine describes God's hardening as his unwillingness to show mercy to sinners.[22]

Following the discussion of hardening in Romans 9, Augustine elaborates on what it means to receive faith by grace

---

[18] Weaver, *Divine Grace and Human Agency*, 5.
[19] Augustine, "Epistle 194," 310.
[20] Augustine, "Epistle 194," 310.
[21] Ogliari, *Gratia et Certamen*, 32.
[22] *Ad Simplicianum* 1.2.15.

without merit. Alluding to 1 Corinthians 4:7 ("For who makes you different from anyone else? What do you have that you did not receive? And if you did receive it, why do you boast as thought you did not?" [NIV]) he asks, "What merit does a man have before faith so as to receive faith?"[23] Wisdom, understanding, counsel, fortitude, knowledge, piety, fear of God, and faith are all gifts from God (Cf. Isaiah 11:2–3). 1 Corinthians 4:7, a favourite text of his, is first used by Augustine in *Ad Simplicianum* and appears in other works like *De peccatorum meritis et remissione ed de baptism parvulorum* (412). Bonner notes the text's importance to Augustine's predestinarianism: some have argued that when Augustine first came to understand the meaning of the text, it was like a Damascus road experience. Bonner doubts this and sees it as "the culmination of a process which had been in progress for several years."[24] This process began in his writings against the Manichaeans and included the writing of *De libero arbitrio*. Augustine references the passage in *Enarratio in Psalmum* 3.3 (394–395) and it appears in *De Diversis Quaestionibus octaginta tribus* (388/396). In each, though, it does not have the same connotations as *Ad Simplicianum*. In the latter Augustine saw that faith is included in Paul's use of the

---

[23] Augustine, "Epistle 194," 310.
[24] Bonner, *Freedom and Necessity*, 43.

phrase "all things." In *De praedestinatione sanctorum* 4 he says, "God revealed this to me when, as I said, I was writing to bishop Simplician on the resolution of this question" of faith. The meaning of the text came after reading Cyprian who "put this whole issue under the title, 'We must boast over nothing since we have nothing of our own.'"[25] "All things" includes faith but this "does not permit any of the faithful to say: I have faith which I have not received."[26] His understanding of the reception of faith based upon 1 Corinthians 4:7 leads him, in *Epistula* 194, to consider the role of faith that is similar to his later discussion of the *initium fidei*—the hub of the controversy with the monks in Hadrumetum.[27] Augustine says

> that faith itself is not to be attributed to the human free will which these men extol, nor to any antecedent merits, since any good merits, such as they are, come from

---

[25] Augustine, *The Predestination of the Saints* in Roland J. Teske trans., *Answer to the Pelagians, IV: To the Monks of Hadrumetum and Provence* in *The Works of Saint Augustine: A Translation for the 21st Century* 1.26 (Hyde Park, New York: New City Press, 1999), 155.

[26] Augustine, *The Predestination of the Saints*, 155.

[27] Marianne Djuth, "Initium Fidei" in Allan D. Fitzgerald ed., *Augustine Through the Ages: An Encyclopedia* (Grand Rapids, MI/Cambridge, UK: Wm. B. Eerdmans, 1999), 447–451.

faith; but we must confess it is a free gift of God, if we are thinking of true grace without merit.[28]

Good works are given to and performed by humans, but faith is imparted irrespective of them. Good works include human acts such as prayer, which is itself an act of faith: "It is faith that prays ... for if it were not given he could not pray."[29] Later he says that prayer does not produce merit, but every prayer is counted among the gifts of grace.[30] Prayer is truly a human action that is freely offered to God, but is preceded by faith and aided by the Spirit. "The help of the Spirit," Augustine says, "is described by saying that He does what He makes us do."[31] The Spirit helps the believers to rightly believe and also to profitably pray.[32] It is by prayer that faith comes to the believer, which "in His love has been graciously imparted to us by the operation of prayer."[33]

Preaching, like prayer, is also a good work. "The 'minister of Christ,' the preacher of this grace, 'because of the grace which is given to him,' is the one who plants and waters

---

[28] Augustine, "Epistle 194," 307.
[29] Augustine, "Epistle 194," 307.
[30] Augustine, "Epistle 194," 311.
[31] Augustine, "Epistle 194," 311.
[32] Augustine, "Epistle 194," 312.
[33] Augustine, "Epistle 194," 321.

The Theology of *Epistula* 194

... 'but God [gives] the increase.' "[34] Many who hear—but not all—are given faith. Augustine explains the mystery of this reality by again appealing to Romans 9:

> The reason why one believes and another does not believe, although both hear the same thing, and, if a miracle is worked in their sight, both see the same thing, is hid in the depth of the riches of the wisdom and of the knowledge of God whose judgments are unsearchable, and with whom there is no injustice, when He 'has mercy on whom He will and whom He will He hardeneth,' for his judgments are not unjust because their meaning is hidden.[35]

Faith draws sinners to Christ and is given as a free gift; not based on a fore-seeing.[36] No person could come to God

> [U]nless it were given him by the Father, and consequently also by the Son Himself and by the Holy Spirit.

---

[34] Augustine, "Epistle 194," 307. For more on Augustine and preaching see Peter T. Sanlon, *Augustine's Theology of Preaching* (Minneapolis, MN: Fortress Press, 2014) and Ian Hugh Clary, "'By Piety in Prayer': Augustine and the Preaching of Scripture," *Reformation Today* 286 (November-December 2018): 29–33.

[35] Augustine, "Epistle 194," 308.

[36] Augustine, "Epistle 194," 309.

GOD CROWNS HIS OWN GIFTS

There is no separation in the gifts and works of the inseparable Trinity; when the Son thus honors His Father He does not give us proof of any separation, but He does offer us a great example of humility.[37]

Eternal life is also a gift of grace, even though it is awarded based upon merits antecedent to death. The merits for which eternal life are awarded "are not effected by us through our sufficiency, but are effected in us by grace." Augustine cites Romans 6:23 to prove that the wages of sin is death, "but the grace of God life everlasting in Christ Jesus our Lord."[38] When Paul speaks of the wages of sin being death he does not say that the wages of justice is eternal life. The idea of payment is used frequently in Scripture, but never in relation to justice or faith. Wages are something owed, but grace is something freely given. Instead of speaking of wages concerning eternal life, Paul speaks of grace.[39] "Faith," says Augustine, "has no more salutary doctrines to believe than this because the understanding finds none more true, and we should hearken to the Prophet saying: 'if you will not believe, you shall not understand.'"[40] According to

---

[37] Augustine, "Epistle 194," 309.
[38] Augustine, "Epistle 194," 313.
[39] Augustine, "Epistle 194," 314.
[40] Augustine, "Epistle 194," 314.

The Theology of *Epistula* 194

Weaver, "[T]his faithful life is the reward for the faithful life of the believer. Nevertheless, as this faithful life is the result of God's gracious indwelling, its achievement consists of grace rewarding grace."[41]

Augustine, like Paul, anticipates the challenge that God is unfair when he selects some to eternal life and passes others over to eternal death. Though it is God who chooses to save, those who are left to perdition are yet without excuse. Augustine quotes Romans 9:20, "O man, who are thou that repliest against God?"[42] Even those who are "ignorant" of their sin and the remedy for it are without excuse; the root of ignorance is not lack of knowledge, but human pride. Such *amour propre* (self worth) presumes "on the strength of free will" and "thinks it is excused when its sin seems to come from ignorance, not from a deliberate choice."[43] There is no one who is truly ignorant of God's law, and "a most just punishment falls on those who try to make excuses for their sins and wickedness." Only grace delivers one from such arrogance and ignorance.[44]

Augustine's final statement on grace and merit in *Epistula* 194 concerns baptism; paedobaptism proves that God is

---

[41] Weaver, *Divine Grace and Human Agency*, 5.
[42] Augustine, "Epistle 194," 316.
[43] Augustine, "Epistle 194," 317.
[44] Augustine, "Epistle 194," 319.

not a respecter of persons.[45] An infant must be born again of water and the Holy Spirit, which Augustine says occurs at baptism. Baptism is the "laver of regeneration" by which the infant enters into the kingdom.[46] Therefore, baptism underscores the gratuitous character of grace because there are some children who are not baptized before premature death and go to hell. Children who are baptized before death—even of unbelieving parents—enter the kingdom of God. Baptism effects regeneration because it eradicates original sin in the infant. In Augustine's words,

> Yet, the providence of God, by which the hairs of our head are numbered, without whose will not a sparrow falls to the ground, which is neither constrained by fate, nor restrained by chance happenings, nor frustrated by an injustice, does not provide rebirth to a heavenly inheritance for all the children of His sons, yet does provide it for some children of evil men.[47]

---

[45] Augustine, "Epistle 194," 321. For a fuller treatment by Augustine on the sacrament see *De baptismo* (ca. 400-401), though it deals primarily with the issue related to the Donatist controversy. An excellent study of Augustine on baptism is David F. Wright, "Augustine and the Transformation of Baptism" in David F. Wright ed., *Infant Baptist in Historical Perspective: Collected Studies* Studies in Christian History and Thought (Milton Keynes, UK: Paternoster, 2007), 68-88.

[46] Augustine, "Epistle 194," 322.

[47] Augustine, "Epistle 194," 322.

The Theology of *Epistula* 194

Bonner says, with a degree of revulsion, "Augustine was to concede that unbaptized infants would suffer the mildest penalties in hell and that the degree of penal suffering by the damned would be proportionate to the quality of their offenses."[48] In the history of baptismal development, David F. Wright comments on the role of Augustine at this period:

> Augustine's early writings show that he, like other Christians of his time, had done little theological thinking about infant baptism. On baptism they are neither passionate nor profound. A new clarity came to his treatment of baptism after c.410 in his anti-Pelagian writings ... The result was a devaluation of baptism in the West which did much to determine the contours of Christendom.[49]

The rest of the text continues Augustine's theology of infant baptism that goes beyond the purpose of this essay.

To conclude, the formal theme of the *Epistula* 194 is the rejection of the Pelagian teaching on the relationship of grace to human merit. This is a polemical piece that intends to drive the Pelagians from their last *Festung*. Invincible grace is the overwhelming theme, in particular as it governs human

---

[48] Bonner, *Freedom and Necessity*, 13.
[49] Wright, "Augustine and the Transformation of Baptism," 68.

merit. Though Augustine grants that the will is free, the freedom to will the good is possible only in light of the prior reception of God's gratuitous grace that changes the human will.

4

"The Grace of God With Him": The Theology of *De gratia et libero arbitrio*

Epistula 194 sent the monastic community in Hadrumetum into confusion. After its roundabout reception a debate erupted with some monks on the one side who over-emphasized Augustine's teaching on grace and those on the other who rejected it. When Augustine heard of the trouble he set to remedy it by writing *De gratia et libero arbitrio*. In it Augustine hopes to allay fears that grace quashes free choice. As Weaver observes, "Augustine's stance, as might be expected, affirmed the necessity of both grace and free will but with far greater emphasis on grace."[1] Yet, of the four treatises in the so-called "semi-Pelagian" controversy "this first one has the greatest emphasis on human responsibility."[2]

Roland J. Teske, the editor of a recent translation, divides the work into two parts:

---

[1] Rebecca Harden Weaver, *Divine Grace and Human Agency: A Study of the Semi-Pelagian Controversy* (Macon, GA: Mercer University Press, 1996), 16.

[2] Weaver, *Divine Grace and Human Agency*, 17.

The Theology of *De Gratia et Libero Arbitrio*

The first part is a scriptural proof of the existence of free choice and of the necessity of divine grace (paragraphs 2–22). The second part is an explanation of the doctrine of grace (paragraphs 23–45) and a conclusion (paragraph 46).[3]

For the sake of space and for the purpose of determining the use of free choice in the treatise, a detailed summary of the first principal part will be offered. In terms of structure and content the second principal part mirrors quite significantly *Epistula* 194. It deals almost completely with grace, and therefore will be summarized more generally.

In the introduction Augustine explains to the abbot Valentinus, the recipient, why he writes:

[B]ecause there are some who defend the grace of God so that they deny the free choice of human beings or who think that free choice is denied when grace is defended, I have undertaken, because our mutual love compels me, to write something on this topic for Your Charity.[4]

---

[3] Roland J. Teske, "General Introduction" in Roland J. Teske trans., *Answer to the Pelagians, IV: To the Monks of Hadrumetum and Provence* in *The Works of Saint Augustine: A Translation for the 21st Century* 1.26 (Hyde Park, NY: New City Press, 1999), 14.

[4] Augustine, "Grace and Free Choice" in Roland J. Teske trans., *Answer to the Pelagians, IV: To the Monks of Hadrumetum and Provence* in *The Works of Saint Augustine: A Translation for the 21st Century* 1.26 (Hyde Park, NY: New City

GOD CROWNS HIS OWN GIFTS

The first part contains two subsections. In the first are proofs offered from scripture for the existence of free will (paragraphs 2–6). Much as he explained in *Epistula* 194, the sinner cannot be excused for sin based on a plea of ignorance. God has revealed his will in three ways: in the creation of the world; through the law; and through Christ. Because of the clarity of this three-fold revelation, the sinner is left without excuse. Augustine says, "They lose this excuse when they receive the commandment or when they are presented with the knowledge that they should not sin."[5] Some try to excuse themselves by declaring God to be unjust in his judgment. This, for Augustine, is to no avail because God is absolutely just (paragraph 3). He appeals to James 1.13–15 where the apostle says that no one can claim to be tempted by God. The foolish man in Proverbs 19:3 accuses God in his heart: "The folly of a man spoils his ways: and he blames God in his heart" (LXX). In the advice of the extra-canonical Sirach 15:11–18, "Do not say, 'He himself led me to it.'" All of this proves that the "free choice of the human will" is clearly expressed.[6]

Press, 1999), 71. Henceforth this text will be quoted Augustine, "Grace and Free Choice."

[5] Augustine, "Grace and Free Choice," 72.
[6] Augustine, "Grace and Free Choice," 72.

The Theology of *De Gratia et Libero Arbitrio*

In paragraph 4, echoing certain Pelagian concerns, ironically, Augustine shows that the commandments of God presuppose free will. When God commands something it is possible to obey or disobey. Augustine lists commands from the Old Testament and from the New that are undergirded by Latin prohibitions such as *ne dimittas* (Proverbs 1:8), *ne moliaris* (Proverbs 3:39), *nolite thesaurizare* (Matthew 6:19) and *nolite peccare* (1 Corinthians 15:34). "Where it says, 'Do not do this,' and 'Do not do that,' and where in God's counsels the act of the will is required for doing or for not doing something, the existence of free choice is sufficiently proven."[7] Even those without the law are without excuse because of their natural understanding (paragraph 5). Romans 2:12 says all who have sinned, whether under the law or apart from the law, are justly condemned. According to Augustine, Paul "said this about the Gentiles and about the Jews, for the former are apart from the law, while the latter received the law." Although the one with the greater knowledge will receive the greater punishment for sin, all are still under the just condemnation of the law. Ignorance "exempts no one from burning in everlasting fire … though such a person perhaps burns in a gentler flame."[8] Because the existence of free

---

[7] Augustine, "Grace and Free Choice," 73–74.
[8] Augustine, "Grace and Free Choice," 74.

will is evident in scripture, one does not have to deny free grace in order to defend free choice (paragraph 6).

After demonstrating the biblical ground for free will, Augustine turns in the second subsection to prove from scripture that "grace is absolutely necessary for our making good use of our free choice."[9] First, grace is necessary for maintaining "marital chastity" (paragraph 8) as well as for overcoming temptation (chapter 9).[10] Each person is to pray that they may not enter into temptation (Matthew 26:41); such a prayer is a free act of the will. In answer to prayer, "A human being is then helped by grace in such a way that his will does not receive the commandments at no purpose."[11]

There are three stages in the Christian life where grace is needed to aid free choice. The first is conversion (paragraph 10–11), which Augustine describes as a "turning to God" based upon Zechariah 1:3. Turning to God pertains to the will, but is accompanied by the grace of God "turning to us." This mutual turning is not the fraudulent Pelagian idea that

---

[9] Teske, "General Introduction," 14.

[10] Augustine, "Grace and Free Choice," 76; the appropriate example of chastity was relevant to the monastic experience.

[11] Augustine, "Grace and Free Choice," 77.

The Theology of *De gratia et libero arbitrio*

the "grace of God is given in accord with our merits." Rather, "our turning to God [is] itself a gift of God."[12] In paragraph 12 Augustine gives Paul as an example of one whose merit did nothing to earn him favour with God. In 1 Corinthians 15:9, Paul's merit was evil, but he explains how "he was repaid with good in return for evil." The grace of God helped Paul in his free choice when he was converted. Augustine says, basing his words on 1 Corinthians 15:10, "And for this reason it was neither the grace of God alone nor the Apostle alone, but the grace of God with him."[13]

The second stage of the Christian life concerns good works performed after salvation (paragraph 13). Grace is required just as much for the performance of good works as it is for conversion. Just as the grace of God is required for conversion, it is also required for good works:

> [O]nce grace has been given, our good merits also begin to exist, but through that grace. For, if grace is withdrawn, a human being falls, no longer standing upright, but cast headlong by free choice. Hence, even when a human being begins to have good merits, he ought not to attribute them to himself, but to God.[14]

---

[12] Augustine, "Grace and Free Choice," 77–78.
[13] Augustine, "Grace and Free Choice," 79.
[14] Augustine, "Grace and Free Choice," 79.

GOD CROWNS HIS OWN GIFTS

Grace is what is needed in the justification of the sinner. Once a person has been justified by faith, "he needs grace to walk with him so that he may lean on it in order not to fall."[15] To prove this, Augustine appeals to 2 Timothy 4:6-8 where Paul says to Timothy,

> If you point these things out to the brothers and sisters, you will be a good minister of Christ Jesus, nourished on the truths of the faith and of the good teaching that you have followed. Have nothing to do with godless myths and old wives' tales; rather, train yourself to be godly. For physical training is of some value, but godliness has value for all things, holding promise for both the present life and the life to come (paragraph 14).

In this Paul, near death, speaks of his accomplishments as the "good merits" that anticipate the gaining of the crown in glory. These merits were given to Paul who before his conversion only had "evil merits." In light of Paul's words Augustine asks, "Would the just judge give him the crown if the merciful Father had not given him grace? And how could this

---

[15] Augustine, "Grace and Free Choice," 80. For Augustine's doctrine of justification see David F. Wright, "Justification in Augustine" in Bruce L. McCormack ed., *Justification in Perspective: Historical Development and Contemporary Challenges* (Grand Rapids/Edinburgh: Baker Academic/Rutherford House, 2006), 55-72.

be the crown of justice unless it was preceded by the grace which makes the sinner just? How could this crown be given as something owed unless that grace had first been given as gratuitous?"[16]

The third stage is eternal life. In paragraph 15 Augustine explains the Pelagian view that eternal life is given according to works. As in *Epistula* 194, Augustine cites 1 Corinthians 4:7 as a text against the Pelagians and forms the crux of Augustine's argument in *De gratia et libero arbitrio*. Paul asks "What do you have that you have not received?" God gives even the merit that the Pelagian thinks earns eternal life. The very ability to do good works is a gift. In response Augustine declares, "God crowns his gifts, not your merits, if your merits come from yourself, not from him." If merit comes from the person without regard to God, they are "evil merits" and God does not crown them. If the merits are a gift from God, they are "good." Augustine reiterates, "If, then, your good merits are God's gifts, God does not crown your merits as merits, but as his own gifts."[17] Augustine uses Paul, who fought the good fight and ran the race, as an example of keeping the faith which is by God's grace (paragraph 16–18). The race depends on God, who gives faith as a gift. Although

---

[16] Augustine, "Grace and Free Choice," 80.
[17] Augustine, "Grace and Free Choice," 81.

works are important for salvation—faith is not bare—they are from God.[18] "Because we have our good works from God from whom we have both faith and love, the same teacher of the nations also called eternal life itself a grace."[19]

Augustine anticipates the question how eternal life can be considered grace if it is based on works (paragraph 19). In paragraph 20 he answers with a number of biblical texts. Jesus said to the disciples that without him they can do nothing (John 15:5). Paul says salvation is not of works (Ephesians 2:8–9), though in Ephesians 2:10 he says that "we are his work, created in Christ Jesus for good works, which God has prepared in order that we might walk in them." Thus God prepares the works of the Christian beforehand which are then rewarded with eternal life. Augustine gives a logical argument to advance his case:

[I]f our good life is nothing but the grace of God, eternal life, which is a recompense for our good life is undoubtedly also the grace of God. For eternal life is also given gratuitously because the good life for which it is given is given gratuitously. But the good life to which eternal life is given is only grace; the eternal life, however, which is given for it, because it is its reward, is

---

[18] Augustine, "Grace and Free Choice," 82.
[19] Augustine, "Grace and Free Choice," 83.

grace in return for grace, as a recompense for righteousness. In that way it may remain true—for it is true—that God 'will repay each according to his works' (Matt. 16:27; Rom. 2:6; Ps. 62:13).[20]

In paragraph 21 Augustine shows that though God repays "grace in return for grace" (Cf. John 1:16), free choice is preserved. God gives eternal life, "not in return for our merits, but out of his mercy." By giving good works God "challenges their free choice, but they are to work 'with fear and trembling' so that they do not become filled with pride over their good works, as if they were their own, by attributing to themselves the good they do." While good works are an act of the will, such an act is possible as the gift of God.[21]

In closing the first principal part on free choice in paragraph 22, Augustine segues into the second on grace by discussing the relationship between the law and grace. God commands Christians to do good by the exercise of free choice and not do evil because this is what the law commands. In human hearts the law produces anger because it is impossible to keep. Augustine quotes Romans 3:20—no flesh will be found righteous on the basis of law because knowledge of sin comes through the law. He distinguishes

---

[20] Augustine, "Grace and Free Choice," 84.
[21] Augustine, "Grace and Free Choice," 85.

between the old condition where the law produces anger and the new condition of the Spirit that sees the law as holy and sin is seen as sin (Romans 7:7-13). This gracious condition of the Spirit allows the sinner to be justified apart from the law (Galatians 2:16).

The second principal part examines the nature of grace to help his initial audience understand it in light of what has been said about free choice. Augustine starts with a threefold negative statement of what grace is not. This takes up the first section of paragraphs 23 to 27. First, grace is not the law (paragraph 23), which the Pelagians argue. If grace were law each person would be the source of his or her own righteousness (paragraph 24). Second, human nature was not created as grace, though the faculties of mind and will are a gift from God. Human nature cannot be grace because unbelievers share in this nature (paragraph 25), but have not received grace. Third, grace is not only forgiveness of sins, but is also the ability to resist temptation to future sin (paragraph 26). The Pelagians, who are confronted with the scripture proof that grace is not given in accord with good works, argue that grace is given in accord with the merit of will (paragraph 27).

The second section, paragraphs 28 to 39, argues for the gratuitous character of grace with a host of scripture texts. One text, Ezekiel 11, in which God takes away the heart of stone and replaces it with a heart of flesh, shows that conversion is a gift of God. In paragraph 31 Augustine looks at free grace in relation to the possibility of obeying God's commandments. He provides a list of texts where God shows that he expects his commandments to be followed (Psalm 95:8; 80:4; 84:4; Ezekiel 18:31–32; 36:26; Romans 4:5; Sirach 15:16 LXX). This list presupposes the existence of free choice, because freedom is needed to obey. He explains how the ability to follow the commands of God is possible in paragraph 32. God must first prepare the will so that "we do what we will." This preparation comes only through prayer. The will, by which one does the will of God, is summed up by love as expressed in 1 Corinthians 12–14 (paragraphs 33– 36). This love is God's gift (paragraph 37), as the ability to love God is rooted in God's first loving sinners (paragraph 38). That it is a gift from God is proven by a series of texts that show how God has poured love into the hearts of believers through the Holy Spirit (Romans 5:3–5; 2 Timothy 1:7; paragraph 39).

The third and final section, paragraphs 41 to 46, speaks not only of how God directs the will and changes it from bad to good, but also directs it to good actions (paragraph 41). Movement of the will from bad to good is produced in the human heart by God (paragraph 42), who inclines it to the good by mercy and to evil by justice (paragraph 43). Turning to a discussion of infants, Augustine argues, as he did in *Epistula* 194, that infants who die without baptism will be condemned, while those who are given the "bath of rebirth" enter the kingdom of God (paragraph 44). Infants who die without baptism receive God's justice and those who die after baptism receive mercy (paragraph 45).

The concluding paragraph 46 is a plea to his audience to read and re-read his work all the while praying for understanding. Augustine recognises that what he has taught is hard to absorb and requires diligent and prayerful study.

Concluding Comparison

It is clear, even from a cursory reading of *Epistula* 194 and *De gratia et libero arbitrio,* that each have their own soteriological theme. *Epistula* 194 is concerned with the nature of grace against the Pelagian notion that God grants it based upon human merit. For Augustine, grace is gratuitous and is conditioned on nothing but the pleasure of the God who gives it. While *De gratia et libero arbitrio* examines the nature of grace, it is subsumed under the subject of free choice. Augustine answers the question asked at a monastery in Hadrumetum, "How does free choice relate to invincible grace?" The answer is that while every act performed by a human being is truly free, each is predicated by grace. This is especially so in the case of salvation where grace is the primary action that changes the nature of the will so that free choice can now be made for the good. The free acts are given by God, and then are rewarded, or "crowned," so that even the works that please God are a gift from God. Therefore, the statements made by historians like Weaver and Ogliari that assume this distinction between grace and free will are theologically true. *Epistula* 194 is concerned to discuss free grace to such an extent that if read out of context free choice appears to be annihilated. Augustine recognized this as it was brought to his attention, and so *De gratia et libero arbitrio* goes a long way to balancing out his teaching on grace. This study now must turn from questions of theological content to questions of historical background in order to account for this shift in Augustine's emphasis.

5

Augustine the Pastor-Theologian

The following surveys the events of the Pelagian controversy as it involved Augustine, *Epistula* 194, and *De gratia et libero arbitrio* with the purpose to build a contextual framework for his treatment of the monks to whom he wrote the latter treatise. From this a clearer perspective can be offered as to why he wrote as he did, strongly affirming grace on the one hand and free will on the other.

Pelagianism: Historical Background

After the fall of Rome in 410, many who fled in fear came to Africa as refugees, including the British monk Pelagius (*fl.* 400-420).[1] Pelagius had been in Rome and served various churches as an influential layman, interacting with bishops and monks who travelled through the city.[2] His reading of

---

[1] Peter Brown, *Augustine of Hippo: A Biography* (Berkeley/Los Angeles, California: University of California Press, 2000), 341; for more on Pelagius see Brown, "Pelagius and His Supporters"; Robert F. Evans, *Pelagius: Inquiries and Reappraisals* Studies in Pelagius (New York: Seabury Press, 1968), 66-89.

[2] Brown, *Augustine of Hippo*, 341.

The Pastor-Theologian

Paul was published in *Expositions of the Letters of St. Paul*.[3] Pelagius was a good writer and won the respect even of Augustine early on. Pelagius made his views known through letters he wrote to important Christians, such as that addressed to a nun named Demetrias in 413. In it Pelagius argued that it was possible for a man, in this life, to obtain perfection.[4] He based his argument on God's demand for perfection, which implied the ability to attain it. Perfection must be available because Pelagius believed that "man's nature had been created for such perfection to be achieved."[5] Pelagian influence was felt in North Africa by Pelagius' disciple Caelestius. When seeking to become a priest in Carthage—Augustine's domain—Caelestius was quickly condemned. In an early response to Pelagius Augustine referred to him and his followers as "my brothers" whom he exhorted as "friends." In fact, he told the hearers of a sermon to "deal

---

[3] Alexander Souter, *Pelagius's Expositions of the Thirteen Epistles of St. Paul* 3 vols. Texts and Studies IX (Cambridge: Cambridge University Press, 1922–1931).

[4] Jerome saw Pelagius' perfectionism as a revival of "Origenism;" this formed the basis of his critique of Pelagianism that was markedly different than Augustine's; Evans, *Pelagius*, 66.

[5] Brown, *Augustine of Hippo*, 342.

with them in a friendly and fraternal way."[6] This was soon to change.

Peter Brown says that the difference between Augustine and the Pelagians lies in two "radically different views" on the relationship between man and God.[7] The Pelagians were moral reformists who sought to bring themselves into God's favour by their own hard work. The Pelagian ethic was directed not only to themselves as individuals, but the church as a whole. As Brown notes: "Pelagius wanted every Christian to be a monk."[8] Such was not unfamiliar to Augustine, who as a young Christian believed that Christians could achieve a measure of perfection sought through monastic life. Now, as a bishop he recognised that perfection was a hope not to be met this side of eternity. Agostino Trapè sees three phases to Augustine's interaction with the Pelagians that correspond with the three groups he challenged. The first involved Pelagius directly along with Caelestius; the second with Julian of Eclanum; and the third, though not

---

[6] Augustine, "Sermon 294" quoted in Agostino Trapè, *Saint Augustine: Man, Pastor, Mystic* (New York: Catholic Book Publishing Corp., 1986), 197-198.

[7] Brown, *Augustine of Hippo*, 352. Robert Evans, however, nuances the debate over Pelagius and Augustine, by highlighting orthodox statements of the former, and setting them in its overall religious and political context.

[8] Brown, *Augustine of Hippo*, 348.

strictly Pelagian, was Augustine's interaction with the monks of Hadrumetum and Gaul.⁹

Robert Evans suggests that Augustine's official entrance into the debate with Pelagius occurred in 415 with the publication of *De natura et gratia*, a critique of Pelagius' now lost *De Natura*, though Augustine does not mention Pelagius in the treatise.¹⁰ In his broader work Augustine showed concern with the Pelagian inability to account for evil. The Pelagian believed that "if human nature was essentially free and well-created, and not dogged by some mysterious inner weakness, the reason for the general misery of men must be somehow external to their true selves."¹¹ This freedom was a terrible weight on the sinner who was responsible for every action and sin; there was no remission but by the work of their own will. James Wetzel says that Augustine "neatly reduces Pelagianism to three grave errors." First, that God's redemption is based on human merit; second, that some humans can attain perfection before God; third, the possibility of perfection is predicated on the denial that Adam's sin is imputed

---

⁹ Trapè, *Saint Augustine*, 198. Based on these representative Pelagians, Evans also wants to keep in mind that Pelagianism was not a monolith, and that each figure's thought must be regarded on its own terms, Evans, *Pelagius*, 68.

¹⁰ Evans, *Pelagius*, 70.

¹¹ Brown, *Augustine of Hippo*, 350. It would appear that Augustine, and Pelagius, are both concerned with refuting Manichaeism in their respective treatments on evil. Evans, *Pelagius*, 68.

GOD CROWNS HIS OWN GIFTS

to the sinner.[12] Bonner reduces Augustine's complaint with the Pelagians to one error: that the Pelagians asserted a human "independence of God, which left no need for efficacious grace."[13]

In December 415 a synod met in Diospolis to consider Pelagianism. Pelagius was present and took the opportunity to distance himself from Caelestius and to lessen the brunt of some of his more extreme statements. The council gave Pelagius a positive ruling and a clean slate.[14] In response, the church in North Africa, led by Augustine, held its own council in Carthage in September 416 and condemned Pelagius

---

[12] James Wetzel, "Predestination, Pelagianism, and foreknowledge" in Eleonore Stump and Norman Kretzmann eds., *The Cambridge Companion to Augustine* (Cambridge: Cambridge University Press, 2001), 52.

[13] Bonner, *Freedom and Necessity*, 3. Evans argues that Augustine reacted against Pelagius's *On Nature* "because he finds there a whole section in which Pelagius has supported his own position by quoting from works of weighty Catholic authors: Lactantius, Hilary of Poitiers, Ambrose, John Chrysostom, Xystus the Martyr bishop of Rome, Jerome, and finally Augustine himself. Pelagius becomes a serious threat at that moment when Augustine sees him marshaling the forces of Catholic orthodoxy behind him. Of one thing Augustine was certain— that on the important doctrines of sin, grace, and freedom he spoke with no other voice than that of the Catholic Church." Evans, *Pelagius*, 85. In Augustine's interaction with Pelagius one thinks of the statement by Christopher Hitchens: "The test of a well-conducted argument is not its ability to convert or to persuade. It lies in is capacity to refine or redefine the positions of the other side." Christopher Hitchens, "Introduction" in *Left Hooks, Right Crosses: A Decade of Political Writing*, ed. Christopher Caldwell and Christopher Hitchens (New York: Nation Books, 2002), 211.

[14] Brown, *Augustine of Hippo*, 357–358.

55

and his teaching. It was the council's fear that Pelagius would receive the support of Innocent I in Rome, so they sent the bishop the proceedings of the council in Carthage as well as a selection of Pelagius' writings. Innocent was left to decide between Diospolis and Carthage.[15] On March 12, 417 Innocent died and Zosimus took his place. The new bishop was favourable to the Pelagians and granted them a measure of freedom in Rome. He viewed the debate as an occasion of "hairsplitting."[16] It took the intervention of the Emperor Honorius to decide the matter finally. After a violent episode that involved Pelagian supporters, Honorius expelled Pelagius and Caelestius from Rome. Following suit, Zosimus also ruled against the Pelagians and published *Epistula tractatoria* condemning the Pelagians throughout the Roman world. Pelagius was expelled and disappeared into relative obscurity. Yet for Augustine, the controversy continued. An Italian bishop, Julian of Eclanum (*ca.* 380–454), carried the mantle for the Pelagians and engaged Augustine *tête à tête* in a debate that lasted the duration of Augustine's life.[17]

---

[15] Brown, *Augustine of Hippo*, 359.

[16] Brown, *Augustine of Hippo*, 361.

[17] For more on the dispute with Julian see Alister E. McGrath, "Divine Justice and Divine Equity in the Controversy between Augustine and Julian of Eclanum," *Downside Review* 101 (1983): 312–319.

God Crowns His Own Gifts

The Writing of *Epistula* 194

In 418/419, Augustine wrote to Sixtus (d. 440), a priest in Rome from 432 to 440, and presented his argument against the Pelagians with "great force."[18] This same priest was to become the bishop of Rome, whom later Roman Catholics refer to as pope Sixtus III (sometimes Xystus); a name often associated with the great room in Rome, the Santa Sabina that was dedicated during his reign. More importantly, Sixtus presided over the Council of Ephesus (431) that debated whether Mary should be called *Theotokos* ("God-bearer") and involved Cyril of Alexandria (*ca.* 378–444) and his infamous disputant Nestorius of Constantinople (*ca.* 381–452).[19] More happily, Sixtus was also known for his amicable settlement of a dispute between patriarchs from Constantinople and Antioch, thus bringing about peace between the four major Sees in Christendom, namely the two just mentioned as well as Rome and Alexandria.[20]

---

[18] Rebecca Harden Weaver, *Divine Grace and Human Agency: A Study of the Semi-Pelagian Controversy* (Macon, Georgia: Mercer University Press, 1996), 5.

[19] For debate over Christ's two natures involving Cyril and Nestorius, see John A. McGuckin, *Saint Cyril of Alexandria and the Christological Controversy* (Crestwood, NJ: St. Vladimir's Seminary Press, 2010).

[20] P.C. Thomas, *A Compact History of the Popes* (Mumbai: St. Pauls, 2007), 29.

THE PASTOR-THEOLOGIAN

In his letter Augustine responded to the news that Sixtus finally sided with the orthodox against the Pelagians by refusing to reinstate the recently excommunicated Julian.[21] The news came from Sixtus himself who sent a letter to Carthage after the bishop Zosimus formally condemned Pelagianism. Though Sixtus' letter was brief it "indicated a considerable vigor against the heresy which he was commonly believed to have before defended, and which claimed him as its own."[22] This would have come as a relief to Augustine, as Sixtus had originally sympathized with the Pelagians. However, as Lindsey Anne Scholl argues, based on an examination of moralistic teaching discerned in mosaics commissioned by Sixtus, he never really gave up his Pelagian sympathies.[23] Be that as it may, Augustine initially replied to Sixtus with a short letter, *Epistula* 191, and followed it with the

---

[21] Michael P. McHugh, "Sixtus III" in Everett Ferguson ed., *Encyclopedia of Early Christianity* (New York/London: Garland Publishing Inc., 1990), 854.

[22] Warfield, "Introductory Essay," xlviii–xlix. Barmby also uses the language of "vigour" when discussing Sixtus' correspondence with Augustine. See J. Barmby, "Sixtus III" in Henry Wace and William C. Piercy eds., *A Dictionary of Early Christian Biography: And Literature to the End of the Sixth Century A.D., with an Account of the Principal Sects and Heresies* (1911 ed.; repr. Peabody, MA: Hendrickson Publishers, 1999), 912.

[23] Lindsey Anne Scholl, "The Pelagian Controversy: A Heresy in its Intellectual Context" (unpublished PhD dissertation, University of California Santa Barbara, 2011).

God Crowns His Own Gifts

longer *Epistula* 194.[24] In the latter Augustine wrote to ensure that the Roman priest did not revert to his former error. Both letters, as Warfield goes on,

> urge on Sixtus his duty not only to bring the open heretics to deserved punishment, but to track out those who spread their poison secretly, and even to remember those whom he had formerly heard announcing the error before it had been condemned ... to bring them either to open recantation of their former beliefs, or to punishment.[25]

It was a patristic seek-and-destroy mission. Augustine expresses sorrow that Sixtus may have been sympathetic to the Pelagians: "We had been exceedingly sad when rumor spread abroad the news that you sided with the enemies of Christian grace."[26] The Pelagians had claimed him as being, with Zosimus, on their side.[27] After receiving the letter from Sixtus, "showing forth the candor of your faith," Augustine was "filled with a joy so great that we can more easily contain

---

[24] Augustine, "Epistle 194," 332.

[25] Warfield, "Introductory Essay," xlix.

[26] Augustine, "Epistle 194," 301. Ogliari sees Augustine gently chastising Sixtus' Pelagian past in this statement. Ogliari, *Gratia et Certamen*, 29.

[27] Barmby, "Sixtus III," 912.

The Pastor-Theologian

than describe it."[28] According to Augustine, Sixtus was the "first to pronounce anathema on them [the Pelagians] before a large crowd." Also, by his letter to Aurelius in Carthage, Augustine proved Sixtus' "strong repudiation of their error." Since coming out publicly against the Pelagians, Sixtus now "speaks more openly and comprehensively against that dogma" stating his views on what Paul frequently called "the 'grace of God by Jesus Christ our Lord.'"[29] Augustine explained the joy felt upon the reception of Sixtus' news as a flight of "every shadow … from our hearts." Instead, "such a brilliance of happiness shines there that the former sorrow and fear seem to have intensified the glowing warmth of the joys that were to come."[30]

After his expression of joy Augustine turned to matters of discipline. There were some who "crept into houses" in secret to propagate the teachings of Pelagius. Augustine wanted Sixtus to see to it that such secret teaching was ferreted out and stopped. He encouraged the priest "to follow up by instructing those in whom you have begun … to instill an adequate fear."[31] Some were to be "restrained by severe measures" while others were to be "investigated with care"

---

[28] Augustine, "Epistle 194," 301.
[29] Augustine, "Epistle 194," 302.
[30] Augustine, "Epistle 194," 302.
[31] Augustine, "Epistle 194," 302.

GOD CROWNS HIS OWN GIFTS

and yet others were to be "treated more gently but instructed more diligently." Recognizing that there "may be a fear of their doing harm" he saw that there should be "no backwardness in saving them from harm."[32] This is an example of the reach that ecclesiastical authorities had over the members of their church.

Augustine concludes by asking Sixtus to share any arguments the priest may have discovered so that the bishop might also gain some use from them in his own polemics:

> If you hear that they have thought up other attacks on the Catholic faith, and if you develop any arguments against them, lest they lay waste the weak members of the Lord's flock, in your faithful and truly pastoral charity share them with us.[33]

He wanted any residual Pelagianism in the church to be cleansed, preferably by the teaching of orthodox doctrine. However, Augustine was not averse to the mechanisms of political clampdown with heretics, as in the Donatist controversy, something surely implied in this letter to Sixtus.[34]

---

[32] Augustine, "Epistle 194," 303.

[33] Augustine, "Epistle 194," 332.

[34] Cf. Geoffrey Grimshaw Willis, *Saint Augustine and the Donatist Controversy* (Eugene, OR: Wipf & Stock, 2005).

The Pastor-Theologian

The Writing of *De gratia et libero arbitrio*

In his *Retractationes* Augustine explains his rationale for writing *De gratia et libero arbitrio*: "I wrote the book, on account of those who suppose that free choice is denied when the grace of God is defended and, therefore, defend free choice so that they deny the grace of God, claiming that it is given in accord with our merits." A quarrel arose over the issue of free choice and some monks "were forced to consult me."[35] This quarrel occurred in a monastery in Hadrumetum, the capital of the province of Byzacena, now Sousse (Sūsa), Tunisia. Though a relatively unimportant town when compared to Rome or Milan, it has a storied and interesting past. In the nineth century BC it was a Phoenician colony located in western North Africa and as a port town along the Gulf of Hammamet on the Mediterranean it was important as a prosperous trade route. Hadrumetum also found itself in the fertile region of Sahel, part of the African bread-basket that was so useful to the Romans. Indeed, the town allied itself with Rome during the Punic Wars, though the Carthaginian military commander Hannibal (247–182) made use of it as a base in his campaign against Scipio (236–183) at the end of the

---

[35] Augustine, "Revisions II 66 (93)" in Roland J. Teske trans., *Answer to the Pelagians, IV: To the Monks of Hadrumetum and Provence* in *The Works of Saint Augustine: A Translation for the 21st Century* 1.26 (Hyde Park, NY: New City Press, 1999), 70.

GOD CROWNS HIS OWN GIFTS

Second Punic War.³⁶ The Roman Emperor Trajan (53–117) made it a *colonia*, but by the fifth century AD it was destroyed by the Vandals and left as fragmented communities until Justinian (482–565) rejuvenated it, giving it the apt name of Justinianopolis.³⁷

Though part of a relatively important town, the monastery had little contact with the church at large and the events of the Pelagian controversy passed it by without a whisper.³⁸ In fact Augustine never went to Hadrumetum or the province of Byzacena; the closest he came was the town of Vallis one hundred kilometres away.³⁹

B.R. Rees tells us that "[t]he majority of the monks were simple men, dedicated to the pursuit of the ascetic life and

---

³⁶ Richard A. Gabriel, *Scipio Africanus: Rome's Greatest General* (Washington: Potomac Books, 2008), 176.

³⁷ Edward Lipiński, *Itineraria Phoenicia* Orientalia Lovaniensia Analecta 127, Studia Phoenicia 18 (Leuven, Belgium: Peeters Publishers, 2004), 365–370; Sophrone Pétridès, "Hadrumetum" in *The Catholic Encyclopedia* Vol. 7 (New York: Robert Appleton Company, 1910), online http://www.newadvent.org/cathen/07105b.htm (accessed March 23, 2014).

³⁸ Rebecca H. Weaver, "Hadrumetum" in Allan D. Fitzgerald ed., *Augustine Through the Ages: An Encyclopedia* (Grand Rapids, MI/Cambridge, UK: William B. Eerdmans Publishing Company, 1999), 411–412. See also Jean Chéné, "Introduction" in Jacques Pintard trans., *'Aux moines d'Adrumete et de Provence'* Oeuvres de Saint Augustin 24 3e série, La Grâce (Paris: Desclée de Brouwer, 1962), 44–45.

³⁹ Othmar Perler, *Les voyages de saint Augustin* (Paris: Études Augustiniennes, 1969), 205–405.

The Pastor-Theologian

holding uncomplicated Christian beliefs, so that much of the great battle which had been waged in the more subtle atmosphere of the theologians had passed over their heads almost unnoticed."[40] Likewise, Nora Chadwick, in her telling of the event, recounts it as a charming tale of confused monks stumbling into a theology too advanced for them and needing the help of a wizened old theologian. Though there is something to this quaint perspective, it may not be as quaint as she makes it.[41] The community of monks were described by their abbot as rustic, but they were not all imbeciles. This is important to remember for, as Michael Casiday says,

> An ill-focused attention on putative differences in intellect can keep us from recognising that the earliest stages of the Pelagian controversy in Africa unfolded in an exchange among monks—Augustine in Hippo, Valentine in Hadrumetum, Evodius in Uzala.[42]

The story is related to us in the primary sources where we learn that in 427 a monk named Florus was on a journey from

---

[40] B.R. Rees, *Pelagius: A Reluctant Heretic* (Woodbridge: Boydell & Brewer, 1991), 103 cited in Olgiari, *Gratia et Certamen*, 33.

[41] Nora K. Chadwick, *Poetry and Letters in Early Christian Gaul* (London: Bowes & Bowes, 1955).

[42] Augustine Michael Cortney Casiday, "Tradition and Theology in John Cassian" (unpublished PhD dissertation, University of Durham, 2002), 181.

GOD CROWNS HIS OWN GIFTS

Hadrumetum to his hometown of Uzalis, near the monastery of Augustine's friend Evodius; Augustine's interlocutor in *de libero arbitrio*. Typical of a monk, Florus made good use of Evodius' library, where he found a copy of *Epistula* 194, copied it, and gave it to a monk named Felix to bring back to Hadrumetum. *Epistula* 194 fell like a bomb on the monastery. It was hastily circulated among the monks without prior consent of Valentinus the abbot. These benighted laymen read the letter in horrified wonder; they were mystified by Augustine's teaching on grace—it was their opinion that it destroyed free will, good works, and final rewards. Weaver summarises the bewilderment:

> [T]o the extent that the intervention of divine grace, apart from merit, determines a person's ultimate destiny, the character of a person's actions does not affect that determination. Furthermore, to the extent that grace shapes a person's actions, it is not human agency but the divine operation upon human agency that determines the person's destiny.

For the monks, the monastic ideal rested upon the notion that by one's own agency, coupled with grace, a person can so shape their life according to monastic discipline as "ultimately to attain to God."[43] This adds further credence to the view that not all of the monks were theologically inept. It indicates that at least some were interested in reading theology, and that they understood the potential implications of Augustine's predestinarianism.[44]

Florus returned from Carthage to find the monastery in an apoplectic state and appealed to Valentinus for help. Florus was judged responsible for the disarray and some of the monks "thought that the *Ep*. 194 was a forgery, and that it could not possibly be ascribed to Augustine."[45] Not knowing how to handle the situation, Valentinus turned to Evodius thinking that as he was the owner of the original copy he might have some answers. Evodius' evasively pious reply was to have the concerned monks believe the contents of the letter and pray for understanding. Valentinus turned to another priest named Sabinus who was also of little use. As a last resort Valentinus sent two monks to Hippo to consult with the author of the missive himself, who was now in his

---

[43] Weaver, *Divine Grace and Human Agency*, 1.

[44] Cf. Casiday, "Tradition and Theology," 182–183.

[45] Donato Ogliari, *Gratia et Certamen: The Relationship Between Grace and Free Will in the Discussion of Augustine with the So-Called Semipelagians* (Leuven, Belgium: Leuven University Press, 2003), 34.

seventies. The monks, Cresconius and another Felix, travelled to Hippo with a letter of plight from Valentinus, begging for enlightenment. As Warfield comments, "Now we get a glimpse of life in the great bishop's monastic home."[46]

Augustine, now in the hoary-haired years of life, "warmly" received the monks and listened to how his letter to Sixtus was the cause of such monastic discontent.[47] Not wanting to further the dilemma, Augustine kept the monks with him, taking pains to navigate the shoals of grace and free will in his letter to Sixtus. The monks intended a short stay in Hippo; they wanted to return to Hadrumetum to celebrate Easter. They were, however, overcome by the bishop's hospitality. They opted "to take the opportunity of being in Augustine's presence and of hearing and better understanding his arguments against those whom the bishop of Hippo had labelled as the 'new Pelagian heretics'" (see *Epistula* 215).[48] The prolonged visit gave Augustine the opportunity he desired for their instruction: "he read with them and explained to them not only his letter to Sixtus ... but much of the chief literature of the Pelagian controversy" and the contents of the letter he sent to Valentinus.[49] By this time the first Felix,

---

[46] Warfield, "Introductory Essay," lix.

[47] Ogliari, *Gratia et Certamen*, 37.

[48] Ogliari, *Gratia et Certamen*, 38.

[49] Warfield, "Introductory Essay," lix.

The Pastor-Theologian

who had first circulated the letter amongst the monks, arrived and joined them in sitting under the tutelage of Augustine. When at last they departed, Augustine drafted *De gratia et libero arbitrio* and sent it with a letter to Valentinus, as well as the main documents from the Pelagian controversy, such as the two letters to Innocent I; one from the Council of Carthage and another from the Council of Milevis; accounts of these councils written to Innocent; Innocent's response to the Africans; a letter written to Zosimus; a reply from Zosimus; and the canons from the Council of Carthage.[50]

After receiving the hefty dossier and *De gratia et libero arbitrio*, more objections were sent by confused monks of Hadrumetum. The monks' earlier fears took a practical further step: if what Augustine said about grace was true, then why rebuke another monk if he fell into sin? The only recourse would be to pray for him. So Augustine wrote *De correptione et gratia* to clarify their confusion; Florus returned to Hippo to receive it and be further instructed. Florus, who likely arrived feeling a little timorous, found Augustine suffering poor health, but the bishop received him so that the

---

[50] Teske, "General Introduction," 13. See also Weaver, *Divine Grace and Human Agency*, 15.

monk could in turn give greater clarity when he returned to his monastic community.[51]

As there is no other extant document from the controversy in Hadrumetum, and Augustine offers no further discussion, it is likely that the bishop's labours paid off and the dispute was quelled. This was not necessarily due to them being overawed by his intellectual calibre or his authority as a bishop. Rather, as Casiday observes, "[T]hey ultimately found his explanations congenial because they shared with Augustine in the monastic life, from which Augustine's theology derived and to which it applied."[52] Throughout the ordeal one sees that Augustine is more concerned to pastor the confused monks than to rebuke and excommunicate them as he would have the hardened Pelagians. In *Epistle* 194 he had encouraged Sixtus to take different approaches to Pelagianism, depending on the state of the one who held it. Outright heretics were to be condemned, but those who were weak in the faith were to be "treated more gently but instructed more diligently," he wanted to "save them from harm."[53] After many years he maintained this counsel in his own ministry.

---

[51] Ogliari, *Gratia et Certamen*, 39.
[52] Casiday, "Tradition and Theology," 183.
[53] Augustine, "Epistle 194," 303.

The Pastor-Theologian

The Hadrumatum confusion was no mere theological dispute; it was a matter of pastoral care. This accounts for the tone of *De gratia et libero arbitrio*, and why he went to great lengths to allay their fears that free will was nullified by grace. Augustine the theologian was also Augustine the pastor.

Augustine and the Mentoring Matrix

The blazing light of Augustine the theologian can blind us from seeing him as a bishop in essentially a North African backwater. While he wrote, preached, and taught, he was also concerned with the regular issues of ministry—locally, and in the broader church—and this should not be forgotten.[54] Trapè lists some of the responsibilities that would have been included in Augustine's episcopate:

> A bishop's duties—preaching, catechesis, administration of the sacraments, care of the poor, the defense of the lowly and the underaged, the stewardship of the Church's goods, and above all, the administration of justice—required time, dedication, and energy. In ad-

---

[54] For a general study of Augustine's role as bishop see Frederick van der Meer, *Augustine the Bishop: The Life and Work of a Father of the Church* (London and New York: Sheed and Ward, 1969).

God Crowns His Own Gifts

dition, there was the more wide-ranging task of defending the integrity of the faith against heresy and the unity of the Church against schism.[55]

Augustine describes the burden of ministry in a sermon:

The turbulent have to be corrected, the faint-hearted cheered up, the weary supported; the gospel's opponents need to be refuted, its insidious enemies guarded against; the unlearned need to be taught, the indolent stirred up, the argumentative checked; the proud must be put in their place, the desperate set on their feet, those engaged in quarrels reconciled; the needy have to be helped, the oppressed to be liberated, the good to be given your backing, the bad to be tolerated; all must be loved.[56]

Augustine's apologetic handling of the Pelagian controversy proper, and his later relationship with the monks of

---

[55] Trapè, *Saint Augustine*, 147.

[56] Augustine, "Sermon 340" in Edmund Hill trans., *Sermons 306–340A* Works of St. Augustine: A Translation for the 21st Century (Hyde Park, NY: New City Press, 1994), 293. Paul R. Kolbet, *Augustine and the Cure of Souls: Reviving a Classical Ideal* Christianity and Judaism in Antiquity Series 17 (Notre Dame, Indiana: University of Notre Dame Press, 2010) argues convincingly that Augustine did not merely move from rhetor to theologian at his conversion to Christianity, but maintained the ideals of classical therapy he had utilised as a philosopher at Cassiciacum throughout his ministry in Hippo Regius.

The Pastor-Theologian

Hadrumetum, are both examples of the concrete outworking of these lists. Edward Smither, in his book *Augustine as Mentor*, cites the Hadrumetum controversy as an instance of Augustine's pastoral theology; though the subject is only treated for about half a page, Smither's overall handling of the mentoring influences on Augustine, as well as the methods and means he used to mentor, is relevant to this discussion.[57]

Augustine's mother Monnica (331-387) is the earliest model of mentoring in his life. Throughout *Confessiones* Augustine looked back on her example as a guide for the Christian life, a task she performed alone as her husband Patricius was a pagan and cared little to raise his son according to Christian standards. Smither argues that Monnica mentored Augustine in four ways, mostly before his conversion: through her godly life; her practical faith; her commitment to sound doctrine and practice; and the Christian education she provided in the home.[58] Although Augustine famously deserted her in Carthage to pursue a teaching career in Italy

---

[57] Edward L. Smither, *Augustine as Mentor: A Model for Preparing Spiritual Leaders* (Nashville: B & H Publishing, 2008), 170; see also 158, 212, 237. The following discussion of Augustine and mentoring selects from Smither's sections on the immediate historical context of mentoring in Augustine's day, and the means by which Augustine mentored others.

[58] Smither, *Augustine as Mentor*, 93-100.

GOD CROWNS HIS OWN GIFTS

before his conversion, he later included her in his retreat community in Cassiciacum, northeast of Milan, in 386/387. It was at this time, spent between his conversion and baptism, that he penned what are known as the Cassiciacum Dialogues—*Contra Academicos*, *De beata vita*, and *De ordine*, as well as *Soliloquia*—where Monnica and two others are enjoined in discussion. Monnica was a participant in *De beata vita*, and also administered the affairs of the retreat. The influence of Monnica is clearly felt throughout *Confessiones*, where Augustine commends her faithfulness.[59] She died in Ostia in 387, not long after her son's baptism. John Searle captures Augustine's reaction to her death, based on *Confessiones* 9.12: "When Monica, Augustine's mother died,/Great was his grief, yet he held down the tide/Of climbing sorrow, and allowed no trace/Of tears to fret the stillness of his face."[60] And while this indicates Augustine's stoic mourning, Monnica's abiding legacy shaped him deeply through the remainder of his life.

It is clear that from early on Augustine enjoyed the company of others. Whether it is the flagitious scene from *Confessiones* of a young Augustine stealing fruit with "the

---

[59] See especially *Confessiones* 1.11 and 9.9 in Augustine, *Confessions* trans. R. S. Pine-Coffin (Harmondsworth: Penguin, 1961), 31–32, 194–196.

[60] Searle, "After reading Book IX, Chapter XII of the Confessions" in *Verses from St. Augustine*, 26.

Thrashers," his Manichaean fraternal, or the monastic community that he founded in Hippo, Augustine constantly had an entourage in tow. Augustine's philosophy of friendship is explained in a sermon preached in Carthage some time before 413: "In this world two things are essential: a healthy life and friendship. God created humans so that they might exist and live: this is life. But if they are not to remain solitary, there must be friendship."[61] For Augustine, friendship was a dim looking glass by which to glimpse the divine, an impression of eternity, and a taste of the goodness and fullness of life found in the Creator of all things seen and unseen. Augustine lived in what Donald Burt calls the "friendly society."[62] Such society was the soil where his mentoring relationships grew. Of the cortege who travelled with Augustine throughout his various stages of life, Smither highlights three who played a role in his development. Foremost among them is Alypius of Thagaste, the friend most mentioned in *Confessiones*, who had been a student of Augustine's, and was present at Augustine's conversion in a Milanese garden. Two others are Nebridius and Evodius, the latter figured in two

---

[61] Augustine, "Sermon 299D" cited in Donald X. Burt, *Friendship & Society: An Introduction to Augustine's Practical Philosophy* (Grand Rapids, MI: Wm. B. Eerdmans, 1999), 57.

[62] Burt, *Friendship & Society*, 73–76.

God Crowns His Own Gifts

Augustinian dialogues, *De animae quantitate* and *De libero arbitrio*. As we saw above, Evodius also had a small role to play in the Hadrumetum affair, as he was the first to be contacted by the abbot Valentinus after the initial outbreak of controversy.

After Monnica, the biggest influence on the early Augustine was Ambrose of Milan (ca. 337/340–397), the bishop under whose ministry Augustine was converted.[63] As Augustine wandered from the Christian faith, flitting from Manichaeism to Neoplatonism, he believed Christianity to be a lower-class religion, and the Bible a diffuse book. His sensibilities were shaken after he encountered the impressive preaching of Ambrose whose powerful intellect and eloquent speech surprised him. As with Monnica, Smither breaks down Ambrose's influence on Augustine in four ways: Ambrose's holy example; his ability to properly interpret scripture; the rhetorical delights of his oratory; and his role in Augustine's preparation for baptism—under Ambrose, Augustine became a *competente* (a beggar for baptism) and was eventually baptized by his pastor in a cruciform baptismal

---

[63] For Ambrose's life and thought see D. H. Williams, *Ambrose of Milan and the End of Nicene-Arian Conflicts* (Oxford: Clarendon Press, 1995).

The Pastor-Theologian

tank dug in the ground outside of the church in Milan on Easter 387.[64]

Other important mentoring relationships were those with Simplician, Ambrose's theological teacher and eventual successor in Milan, and the one to whom he wrote on grace and free will; and Valerius of Hippo, Augustine's predecessor, and co-labourer in ministry. Both men provided Augustine with rich intellectual fodder for his growing faith, and the latter, whom Augustine called his "sincerely beloved father," was directly involved in bringing Augustine into the pastorate in 395.[65] As Smither says, the influences on Augustine's early life and ministry were diverse, from a simple and uneducated mother, to an intellectual powerhouse like Ambrose. All the while, he was surrounded by friends who grew in faith with him. It is in this context that Augustine's mentoring programme was birthed and nourished.

---

[64] Smither, *Augustine as Mentor*, 103–109. For a moving account of Augustine's baptism see Brown, *Augustine of Hippo*, 117–118. A fascinating description of Ambrose and baptism can be found in Garry Wills, *Font of Life: Ambrose, Augustine, and the Mystery of Baptism* Emblems of Antiquity (Oxford: Oxford University Press, 2012).

[65] Smither, *Augustine as Mentor*, 116.

God Crowns His Own Gifts

Augustine the Mentor

Before turning to Augustine's pastoral theology in light of the Hadrumetum question, it is important to consider his own method of discipling. As bishop, Augustine was in charge of a large number of North African clerics; Jan Joncas says that a council in Carthage in 411 had 268 Catholic and 279 Donatist bishops in attendance.[66] As Smither notes, "From the time of his ordination as presbyter in 391 until his death in 430, Augustine had relationships with hundreds of clergy in Hippo, in the provinces of North Africa, and beyond."[67] His biographer, Possidius of Calama, recounts his own experience of this:

> I myself know of about ten holy and venerable men of continence and learning, some of them quite outstanding, whom blessed Augustine gave upon request to the various churches. These men, inspired by the ideals of that holy community and being now scattered among the Churches of the Lord, founded monasteries in

---

[66] Jan Michael Joncas, "Clergy, North African," in Allan D. Fitzgerald ed., *Augustine Through the Ages: An Encyclopedia* (Grand Rapids/Cambridge: Wm. B. Eerdmans, 1999), 216.

[67] Smither, *Augustine as Mentor*, 125.

The Pastor-Theologian

their turn; as zeal for the spread of God's word increased, they prepared brothers for the priesthood and then advanced them to other Churches.[68]

With this in mind, how did Augustine discharge so wide a ministry?

Augustine followed the trajectory set out for him in the personal examples noted above. As well, he was a product of his time, and mentored in the vein of bishops like Cyprian of Carthage (d. 258) and Basil of Caesarea.[69] In the "mentoring matrix" of the third and fourth centuries Smither shows that written communication—whether correspondence or books—and church councils as means of training up leaders in the faith were prime. Interface between a bishop and those who ministered under him was also vital. This was often a relationship of reciprocity; the bishop had as much to learn about faith and life from a priest.

It was the bishop's job to teach and model sound doctrine in order to be an example to his disciples. If resources were available, then bishops were to make sure that the best theology was dispersed across all regions under his authority. Some, like Cyprian, mentored from the church, while others,

---

[68] Possidius of Calama, *The Life of Saint Augustine*, The Augustinian Series 1, ed. John E. Rotelle (Villanova: Augustinian Press, 1988), 59.

[69] For this background see Smither, *Augustine as Mentor*, 24–92.

like Pachomius (292–348), from the monastery. Due to the circumstances involved in his own growth in the faith, and the surrounding context of ministry, like-patterns emerge in Augustine's attitude to mentorship. While none of his thoughts were set out systematically, the sheer volume of his writings, correspondence, and eye-witness biographical accounts can help historians piece together his scheme. A general survey of Augustine's approach to discipleship will be given, and in the next discussion of how this relates to the monks in Hadrumetum, more detail will be filled out.

As bishop of Hippo Regius, Augustine had many responsibilities, as noted above. His primary role as he saw it involved what is commonly called the administration of "Word and sacrament"; namely the preaching and teaching of biblical theology, and the administering of the sacraments of baptism and the Eucharist. We have over five hundred sermons of Augustine's preached not only in Hippo, but throughout the region, notably Carthage.[70] This does not include works like *Enarrationes in Psalmos*, a collection of sermons preached between 392 and 418.[71] In terms of the

---

[70] Smither, *Augustine as Mentor*, 129.

[71] For a comprehensive list of Augustine's sermons and bibliographic references to different collections see Éric Rebillard, "Sermones" in Allan D. Fitzgerald ed., *Augustine Through the Ages: An Encyclopedia* (Grand Rapids/Cambridge: Wm. B. Eerdmans, 1999), 773–792. A fantastic study of Augustine on

THE PASTOR-THEOLOGIAN

broader North African church, Augustine was also involved in church councils; initially such councils met annually, but after 407 they were called only as needed, typically in cases of controversy. Smither notes, "The main heretical groups addressed by the church councils of Augustine's day were the Donatists and Pelagians."[72]

Like others from this period, Augustine's center of operations was the *monasterium clericorum* in Hippo. While maintaining a public office, Augustine was a "bishop-monk" who ministered from "within the cloister." As part of this interior ministry, he entertained visitors at the monastery that had been converted from bishop Valerius' home. Smither quotes a section of a sermon where Augustine describes the role of a bishop's home base:

> I arrived at the episcopate. I saw that the bishop is under the necessity of showing hospitable kindness to all visitors and travelers; indeed, if a bishop didn't do that he would be said to be lacking in humanity. But if this custom were transferred to the monastery it would not

---

the Psalms is Jason Byassee, *Praise Seeking Understanding: Reading the Psalms with Augustine* Radical Traditions (Grand Rapids: Wm. B. Eerdmans Publishing Co., 2007).

[72] Smither, *Augustine as Mentor*, 132.

GOD CROWNS HIS OWN GIFTS

be fitting. And that's why I wanted to have a monastery of clergy in the bishop's residence.[73]

Augustine lived in the monastery with fellow church leaders and friends like Evodius and Possidius. From within this community a glimpse of Augustine the mentor can be caught.[74]

As in his public office as bishop, Augustine made teaching of prime importance among his colleagues. Possidius outlines the didactic facet of the monastic community in Hippo:

> While the divine teachings were achieving success, some of the men who were serving God in the monastery with and under the direction of holy Augustine began to be ordained clerics for the Church of Hippo. Thus the truth of the preaching of the Catholic Church became daily better known and more evident, and so did the way of life of these holy servants of God with their continence and austere poverty. Other Churches therefore began eagerly to ask and obtain bishops and clerics from the monastery that owed its origin and growth to this memorable man, with the result that the

---

[73] Augustine, "Sermon 355.2" cited in Smither, *Augustine as Mentor*, 149.

[74] The following section selects some of the principles of mentoring that Smither lays out, but only those that relate to the monks of Hadrumetum; Smither, *Augustine as Mentor*, 148–157.

The Pastor-Theologian

Church was established and consolidated in peace and unity.[75]

Possidius points to the growth and influence of monasteries that had Augustine's imprint: "His legacy to the Church was a very numerous clergy and monasteries filled with men and women vowed to continence under the guidance of their superiors, as well as libraries containing his own books and discourses and those of other holy men."[76] Such quotations show the importance of teaching for Augustine; he gave "regular direction," and left a legacy of theological writing for further use in the church. Those who went out from the monastery to minister in other parts were "men of learning" who "spread the word of God." This involved not only the teaching and application of the faith to the laity, but its defence against heresy. Possidius tells of internal discussions between members of the community, where Augustine, eating with some of the clergy, explained why he diverted from his usual preaching method in a sermon to address Manichaeism. As it turned out, a Manichee named Firmus was in attendance, and upon hearing the sermon, converted to the

---

[75] Possidius, *Life of Saint Augustine*, 59.
[76] Possidius, *Life of Saint Augustine*, 130.

God Crowns His Own Gifts

Catholic faith.[77] Smither says that this "table talk allowed the group to reflect on the day by sharing victories and failures while finding renewed courage and vision to carry on in the work of ministry."[78] Augustine was concerned with the internal issues at the monastery, yet he maintained a practice of hospitality; bishops like Paul Orosius and Eutropius would come to Hippo to learn how to deal with the latest heresies.

Augustine is exceptional among Graeco-Roman thinkers for his prolific output, not merely with formal theological treatises, but sermons and correspondence as well. In this vein Smither highlights Augustine's capacious letter writing as another means by which he mentored, and, quoting Adalbert G. Hamman, says, Augustine "is the most consulted man in the western church."[79] In his correspondence, Augustine could influence a range of issues in the church without having to be everywhere at once. His letters were warm and personal, but they could also be administrative, or theological and polemical.[80] During periods of controversy, as we

---

[77] Possidius, *Life of Saint Augustine*, 71–72.

[78] Smither, *Augustine as Mentor*, 153.

[79] Adalbert G. Hamman, *Études Patristiques: Méthodogie, Liturgie, Histoire, Théologie* (Paris: Beachesne, 1991), 277, cited in Smither, *Augustine as Mentor*, 157.

[80] For more on the role of letters in Augustine's ministry see Coleman M. Ford, "'He Who Consoles Us Should Console You': The Spirituality of the

saw with his letter to Sixtus, Augustine used the quill to further his cause.[81] Thus letter writing was an important means of peer mentoring, particularly in the area of encouraging spiritual growth. Smither cites a number of letters, like those to Profuturus and Quintianus, where Augustine sought to encourage others in the faith.[82] Along with letters, Augustine's books are another written source of mentoring. They were sent to clergy like those at Hadrumetum in order to shape orthodox thinking in the churches. According to his own estimate, Augustine says,

> In so far as leisure is granted me from the work imperatively demanded by the church, which my office specially binds me to serve, I have resolved to devote the time entirely, if the Lord will, to the labor of studies pertaining to ecclesiastical learning; in doing which I think that I may, if it please the mercy of God, be of some service even to future generations.[83]

Word in Select Letters of Augustine of Hippo," *Evangelical Quarterly* 89.3 (2018): 240–257.

[81] Smither cites Augustine's letters to Valentinus as an example of Augustine using letters to mentor others. See Smither, *Augustine as Mentor*, 158 n.179.

[82] Smither, *Augustine as Mentor*, 183.

[83] Augustine, "Letter 151.13" cited in Smither, *Augustine as Mentor*, 185.

GOD CROWNS HIS OWN GIFTS

Smither divides Augustine's writings into three categories: theological/exegetical; apologetic; and spiritual. Coupled with his rhetorical gifts, and his intellectual stature, Augustine's treatises continue to have considerable influence today. Of his spiritual writings, Smither looks to *Confessiones* as an example, noting that it was likely penned at the request of Paulinus of Nola, who wanted to know more about Augustine's spiritual pilgrimage.[84]

A final means of mentoring by Augustine that Smither highlights, and that is relevant to the Hadrumetum situation, is that of personal visitation. Although Augustine traveled from North Africa to Europe in his early life, he disliked travel. After his return to Africa in 388, he never again journeyed by sea. However, as bishop he "logged thousands of kilometres across the provinces of North Africa."[85] His travels involved attending church councils, often in nearby Carthage, preaching tours in other cities, and visiting colleagues in other churches. This afforded the personal presence that his letters could not offer, namely, the immediate clarification of questions posed to him by others. This gave him the chance to have meaningful and friendly interaction with his clerics.

---

[84] Smither, *Augustine as Mentor*, 195.
[85] Smither, *Augustine as Mentor*, 207.

The Pastor-Theologian

With this, and other forms of mentoring discussed, Smither draws some conclusions about Augustine as mentor. First, Augustine was warm and personal with those whom he mentored; this is seen especially in his letters, but also in his personal visitations. Second, Augustine used the strategies he learned from the context both of his upbringing, and the mentoring matrix of the early church. Sometimes he combined these strategies, for instance he would send books and letters as resources, or he would send a letter before traveling to the recipient. Smither says:

> Through Augustine's multifaceted approach to mentoring, he provided spiritual direction and encouragement, rebuke and discipline, practical advice for dealing with church matters, exhortation toward maintaining sound doctrine, as well as theological and exegetical help to teach the Scriptures and fight heresy. In many cases, he was personally available and worked alongside leaders of every rank of clerical office, resourcing them toward fulfilling their ministries to the church.[86]

---

[86] Smither, *Augustine as Mentor*, 212.

God Crowns His Own Gifts

Thoughts About Mentoring and Hadrumetum

In light of this context and the exposition of his approach to mentorship, it is evident that Augustine's pastoral-theological role in the Hadrumetum controversy meshes well with Smither's conclusions about Augustine as mentor. Hadrumetum is, in many respects, a high watermark of the long controversy over grace and human freedom. As Paul's epistles move from the didactic to the practical, the affairs over Pelagianism follow a similar trajectory. The opaque theological controversy with Pelagius and Julian that swelled with the language of grace, will, merit, responsibility, filtered to the laity and showed the practical usefulness of rarefied debate. It was not enough for Augustine to maintain a formal orthodoxy in his churches, rather he set to it that those under his care not only outwardly confessed orthodoxy, but also lived it. He was concerned to show that the monks had every reason to admonish a brother in sin, rather than to just pray for him, because Augustine knew that the integrity of the church and her witness to Christ in a dying world depended on it.

The methods of mentoring that Augustine learned first-hand and displayed in his own ministry were put to good use with his confused monks. From what we have seen about Augustine's own mentoring, a number of parallels can be drawn.

Before drawing these parallels, it should be noted that Augustine's practice of mentoring is predicated on the need for sound doctrine in the church. This he learned early on from Monnica, who taught him the faith from boyhood, progressed through his conversion under the ministry of Ambrose, and matured in his own right. To maintain the purity of the Christian confession is Augustine's overarching concern as bishop, whether for his own monastic community, for Hippo, for the church in the Empire, and even in an out of the way place like Hadrumetum. If we were to ask why Augustine was so motivated as to put himself out for the sake of these uneducated monks, it is in doctrinal fidelity that we find our answer.

An important element of mentoring for Augustine was the face-to-face encounter. While this was not always possible for the busy bishop, especially in his old age, Augustine warmly received the monks who first brought Valentinus' letter to him in Hippo. As we saw, though the monks only intended to stay a short while, Augustine implored them to remain, ultimately to celebrate Easter with him. As Warfield describes it, Augustine "craved" for them to stay so that he might explain his teaching on predestination to them, including the parts of his earlier letter to Sixtus and his other anti-Pelagian writings that they had trouble with. Not only did Augustine host the monks, but Felix, who first discovered *Epistula* 194, also came for instruction. Even in a sickly condition, as when Florus the disruptor of the community later came to him, he still opened his home. Augustine showed care for the monks, enough to meet the monks on their own terms. They were not theologically advanced and so he laboured with them until they came to an adequate understanding of the issues—it is worth noting that he went further than his friend Evodius did with them. A man of Augustine's intellect could have easily become bored with the monks' questions and given them the bare minimum of counsel. Instead, Augustine shows awareness of the monks' theological limitations and carefully brings them to clarity and truth. He models pastoral care for his flock and is not content to rest until the controversy is adequately settled in their minds. The apostle Paul told Timothy that one of the qualifications for being an elder was hospitality (1 Timothy 3:2); the relationship that Augustine forged with the monks is a good practical example of this qualification.

A related part of Augustine's mentoring programme that he put to further use with the monks is his writing ministry, both letters and books. His epistles and theological treatises were decisive in stopping Pelagianism from becoming a received teaching in the church. He wrote to leaders expressing his desires for formal discipline against the Pelagians, and he wrote theological refutations of their work for the sake of a broader audience in the church. These writings he would collect and give to other leaders so that they would be equipped to deal with the heresy. Likewise, Augustine sent letters—*Epistulae* 214, 215, and 215A—to Valentinus in Hadrumetum, and wrote two treatises, the first *De gratia et libero arbitrio*, and the second, to clear up further confusion, *De correptione et gratia*. With these, he also provided documents from the earlier controversy, including letters to various leaders and statements from church councils, all with the equipping and edifying purpose of giving clarity to those who were confused. As an undershepherd of Christ's flock, he went to great lengths to protect both the local and the catholic church from the wolves.

6
Augustine Matters Today

In the beginning of this book I mentioned the relevance of the church fathers for today. Sadly, theologically-driven mentorship by "pastor-theologians" is also underappreciated in the twenty-first century church.[1] As Protestants are growing in their appreciation for the church fathers in terms of their Christology, and especially Augustine's soteriology, let us hope that the vision of a ministry that is deeply grounded in biblical doctrine, and manifests itself in the life of ministry, will also be rediscovered. As I hope it has been shown, Augustine is a great starting point and example for the would-be pastor-theologian. Having surveyed the contents of *Epistula* 194 and *De gratia et libero arbitrio*, relating their different emphases to Augustine's pastoral theology, we have developed a new angle by which we can appreciate him as pastor-theologian. As he wrestled to maintain a balance in his predestinarian thought on grace and freedom, he also sought

---

[1] Thankfully this problem is being addressed, a good example is Colin Marshall and Tony Payne, *The Trellis and the Vine: The Ministry Mind-Shift That Changes Everything* (Kingsford: Matthias Media, 2009).

balance in his approach to various pastoral issues. On the one hand, he dealt strongly with the Pelagians, whom he saw as heretical wolves set to devour the sheep. On the other hand, he dealt kindly and patiently with the monks of Hadrumetum because he saw them as just that: sheep. And he was their undershepherd. Thus, as we have accounted for the difference in emphases in terms of content and tone of his engagement with the Pelagians and then the so-called semi-Pelagians, both historically and pastorally, Augustine's pastoral practice has shown itself to be highly relevant for ministry in the twenty-first century.

Regarding the two documents under review, the reasons for their different emphases on grace and free will are accounted for historically by an exploration of the events that led to the writing to Sixtus as well as the events that warranted interaction with the monks of Hadrumetum. Sixtus had only just come to an Augustinian understanding of grace (though, as we saw, there are questions even about that) and it was Augustine's desire to maintain that perspective in the Roman priest. Therefore, undergirding his letter was a strong polemical aim to ensure that ecclesiastical powers eradicated Pelagianism from the church. The monks in Hadrumetum received quite a different reaction from Augustine; he treated them pastorally. Not viewing them as a source of grief, he sought to smooth out the ruffles in their theology by allaying their fears and maintaining the balance between grace and free will. There were no polemics, only a strong sense of responsibility as a pastor and bishop.

The two documents, though concerned with the same themes of grace and free choice, encapsulate the thinking of Augustine as an anti-Pelagian writer. His concerns throughout the broader controversy were both apologetic and pastoral depending on context. At certain points the documents mirror one another in content—in particular the latter part of *De gratia et libero arbitrio*, which is similar to *Epistula* 194—but Augustine's purposes for writing are different. The question asked in the introduction as to veracity of Weaver and Olgiari's statements on the Hadrumetum writings is thus answered affirmatively. Augustine did indeed "pay greater attention to resisting the denial of the existence of free will"[2] in the Hadrumetum correspondence than he did with Sixtus. Augustine, as a theologian, was concerned that false teaching would corrupt the church. To the monks of Hadrumetum, however, Augustine as a pastor was concerned that technical teaching would confuse his flock. He

---

[2] Donato Ogliari, *Gratia et Certamen: The Relationship Between Grace and Free Will in the Discussion of Augustine with the So-Called Semipelagians* (Leuven, Belgium: Leuven University Press, 2003), 58.

was concerned that his views caused alarm in Hadrumetum; he did everything in his power to rectify the situation. This was done through mentorship and discipling. The monks who spent time with Augustine learned about the differences between grace and free will returned to their monastic community to share what they learned with the other monks. It is hoped that each of these emphases brought to light in this essay will be an encouragement to pastors who can find in Augustine the quintessential example of a pastor-theologian.

Works Cited

Ascol, Tom. "The Pastor as Theologian." *The Founders Journal* 43 (Winter 2001), 1–10.

Augustine. *On the Free Choice of the Will, On Grace and Free Choice, and Other Writings*. Cambridge Texts in the History of Philosophy, ed. and trans., Peter King. Cambridge: Cambridge University Press, 2010.

_____. *Answer to the Pelagians, IV: To the Monks of Hadrumetum and Provence*. The Works of Saint Augustine: A Translation for the 21st Century. Trans., Roland J. Teske, ed., John E. Rotelle. Hyde Park, New York: New City Press, 1999.

_____. "Sermon 340." In *Sermons 306-340A*. Works of St. Augustine: A Translation for the 21st Century, Edmund Hill trans., 292-294. Hyde Park, New York: New City Press, 1994.

Works Cited

_____. *The Retractations* The Fathers of the Church trans., M. Inez Bogan. Washington: Catholic University of America Press, 1968.

_____. *Confessions*, trans. R. S. Pine-Coffin. Harmondsworth: Penguin, 1961.

_____. "Epistle 194." In *Saint Augustine: Letters Volume IV (165–203)*, trans. Wilfrid Parsons, 301-332. New York: Fathers of the Church, Inc., 1955.

Barmby, J. "Sixtus III." In *A Dictionary of Early Christian Biography: And Literature to the End of the Sixth Century A.D., with an Account of the Principal Sects and Heresies*, Henry Wace and William C. Piercy eds., 912. Peabody, Massachusetts: Hendrickson Publishers, 1999.

Bonner, Gerald. *Freedom and Necessity: St. Augustine's Teaching on Divine Power and Human Freedom.* Washington, D.C.: The Catholic University of America Press, 2007.

Brown, Peter. *Augustine of Hippo: A Biography*. Berkeley/Los Angeles, California: University of California Press, 2000.

_____. "Pelagius and His Supporters: Aims and Environment." *Journal of Theological Studies* XIX.1 (April 1968): 93–114.

Burt, Donald X. *Friendship & Society: An Introduction to Augustine's Practical Philosophy*. Grand Rapids, Michigan: Wm. B. Eerdmans, 1999.

Casiday, Augustine Michael Cortney. "Tradition and Theology in John Cassian." Unpublished PhD dissertation, University of Durham, 2002.

Chadwick, Henry. *Augustine of Hippo: A Life*. Oxford: Oxford University Press, 2009.

Chadwick, Nora K. *Poetry and Letters in Early Christian Gaul*. London: Bowes & Bowes, 1955.

Works Cited

Chéné, Jean and Jacques Pintard trans., *'Aux moines d'Adrumete et de Provence.'* Oeuvres de Saint Augustin 24 3e série, La Grâce. Paris: Desclée de Brouwer, 1962.

Clary, Ian Hugh. "'By Piety in Prayer': Augustine and the Preaching of Scripture." *Reformation Today* 286 (November–December 2018): 29–33.

Evans, Robert F. *Pelagius: Inquiries and Reappraisals*. Studies in Pelagius. New York: Seabury Press, 1968.

Fitzgerald, Allan D. ed., *Augustine Through the Ages: An Encyclopedia*. Grand Rapids/Cambridge, Michigan/United Kingdom: Wm. B. Eerdmans, 1999.

Ford, Coleman M. "'He Who Consoles Us Should Console You': The Spirituality of the Word in Select Letters of Augustine of Hippo." *Evangelical Quarterly* 89.3 (2018): 240–257.

Gabriel, Richard A. *Scipio Africanus: Rome's Greatest General*. Washington: Potomac Books, 2008.

Harrison, Carol. "Augustine (353–430)." In *Key Thinkers in Christianity*, Adrian Hastings, Alistair Mason and Hugh Pyper eds., Oxford: Oxford University Press, 2003.

Harrison, Simon. *Augustine's Way Into the Will: The Theological and Philosophical Significance of* De libero arbitrio. Oxford Early Christian Studies. Oxford: Oxford University Press, 2006.

Haykin, Michael A. G. *Rediscovering the Church Fathers: Who They Were and How They Shaped the Church*. Wheaton, Illinois: Crossway Books, 2011.

Hitchens, Christopher. *Left Hooks, Right Crosses: A Decade of Political Writing* ed. Christopher Caldwell and Christopher Hitchens. New York: Nation Books, 2002.

Holmes, Stephen R. *Listening to the Past: The Place of Tradition in Theology*. Grand Rapids, Michigan: Baker Academic, 2002.

Lesousky, Mary Alphonsine. *The* De Dono Perseverantiae *of Saint Augustine: A Translation with An Introduction*

Works Cited

and Commentary Washington, D.C.: The Catholic University of America Press, 1956.

Lipiński, Edward. *Itineraria Phoenicia*. Orientalia Lovaniensia Analecta 127, Studia Phoenicia 18. Leuven, Belgium: Peeters Publishers, 2004.

McGrath, Alister E. "Divine Justice and Divine Equity in the Controversy between Augustine and Julian of Eclanum," *Downside Review* 101 (1983): 312–319.

McHugh, Michael P. "Sixtus III." In *Encyclopedia of Early Christianity*, Everett Ferguson ed., 854. New York/London: Garland Publishing Inc., 1990.

McSorley, Harry J. *Luther: Right or Wrong?* New York/Minneapolis: Newman Press/Augsburg Publishing, 1969.

Ogliari, Donato. Gratia et Certamen: *The Relationship Between Grace and Free Will in the Discussion of Augustine with the So-Called Semipelagians* Bibliotheca Ephemeridum Theologicarum Lovaniensium CLXIX. Leuven: Leuven University Press, 2003.

Perler, Othmar. *Les voyages de saint Augustin.* Paris: Études Augustiniennes, 1969.

Pétridès, Sophrone. "Hadrumetum." In *The Catholic Encyclopedia* Vol. 7. New York: Robert Appleton Company, 1910. http://www.newadvent.org/cathen/07105b.htm.

Piper, John. *Contending for Our All: Defending Truth and Treasuring Christ in the Lives of Athanasius, John Owen and, J. Gresham Machen.* Wheaton, Illinois: Crossway, 2006.

Possidius of Calama, *The Life of Saint Augustine.* The Augustinian Series 1, ed. John E. Rotelle. Villanova, Pennsylvania: Augustinian Press, 1988.

Rist, John M. *Augustine: Ancient Thought Baptized.* Cambridge: Cambridge University Press, 1996.

_____. "Augustine on Free Will and Predestination." *Journal of Theological Studies* 20.2 (1969): 420–447.

Works Cited

Sanlon, Peter T. *Augustine's Theology of Preaching*. Minneapolis, Minnesota: Fortress Press, 2014.

Scholl, Lindsey Anne. "The Pelagian Controversy: A Heresy in its Intellectual Context." Unpublished PhD dissertation, University of California Santa Barbara, 2011.

Searle, John. *Verses from St. Augustine, or Specimens from a Rich Mine*. Oxford: Oxford University Press, 1953.

Smither, Edward L. *Augustine as Mentor: A Model for Preparing Spiritual Leaders*. Nashville: B & H Publishing, 2008.

Souter, Alexander. *Pelagius's Expositions of the Thirteen Epistles of St. Paul* 3 vols. Texts and Studies IX. Cambridge: Cambridge University Press, 1922–1931.

Thomas, P. C. *A Compact History of the Popes*. Mumbai: St. Pauls, 2007.

Trapè, Agostino. *Saint Augustine: Man, Pastor, Mystic*, Spirituality for Today Series IV ed., John E. Rotelle. New York: Catholic Book Publishing, 1986.

van der Meer, Frederick. *Augustine the Bishop: The Life and Work of a Father of the Church*. London and New York: Sheed and Ward, 1969.

Warfield, B. B. "Introductory Essay on Augustin and the Pelagian Controversy." In *Nicene and Post-Nicene Fathers Volume 5: Augustin: Anti-Pelagian Writings* First Series, Philip Schaff ed., xiii–lxxi. Peabody, Massachusetts: Hendrickson Publishers, 2004.

Weaver, Rebecca Harden. *Divine Grace and Human Agency: A Study of the Semi-Pelagian Controversy*, Patristic Monograph Series 15. Macon, Georgia: Mercer University Press, 1998.

Wetzel, James. "Predestination, Pelagianism, and foreknowledge." In *The Cambridge Companion to Augustine*, Eleonore Stump and Norman Kretzmann eds., 49–58. Cambridge: Cambridge University Press, 2001.

Works Cited

Williams, D. H. *Evangelicals and Tradition: The Formative Influence of the Early Church*. Grand Rapids, Michigan: Baker Academic, 2005.

_____. *Ambrose of Milan and the End of Nicene-Arian Conflicts*. Oxford: Clarendon Press, 1995.

Willis, Geoffrey Grimshaw. *Saint Augustine and the Donatist Controversy*. Eugene, Oregon: Wipf & Stock, 2005.

Wright, David F. *Infant Baptist in Historical Perspective: Collected Studies*. Studies in Christian History and Thought. Milton Keynes, UK: Paternoster, 2007.

_____. "Justification in Augustine." In *Justification in Perspective: Historical Development and Contemporary Challenges*, Bruce L. McCormack ed., 55–72. Grand Rapids/Edinburgh: Baker Academic/Rutherford House, 2006.

Subject Index

Alypius of Thagaste, 92
Ambrose, 28, 73, 93, 94,
    105, 122
Arianism, 19, 122
Athanasius of Alexandria,
    18, 19, 119
Baptism, 43, 48, 49, 50,
    65, 91, 93, 94, 97
Basil of Caesarea, 18, 96
Caelestius, 70, 71, 73
Christology, 19, 109
Church fathers, 17, 18, 109
Controversy, 1, 13, 20, 21,
    23, 37, 44, 49, 53, 69,
    74, 79, 81, 82, 85, 86,
    87, 89, 90, 93, 98, 101,
    104, 105, 107, 108, 111
Conversion, 57, 58, 60, 64,
    89, 90, 91, 92, 105
Council of Carthage, 86
Council of Ephesus, 75
Council of Milevis, 86
Cresconius, 85
Cyprian of Carthage, 96
Cyril of Alexandria, 75

Donatism, 10, 98
Easter, 85, 94, 106
Education, 90
Emperor Honorius, 74
Eutropius, 101
Evodius, 26, 82, 83, 84,
    92, 98, 107
Excommunication, 87
Felix, 83, 85, 106
Firmus, 100
Florus, 83, 84, 86, 106
Free will, 2, 19, 20, 21, 22,
    23, 24, 25, 28, 29, 32,
    34, 35, 37, 38, 44, 48,
    53, 54, 55, 56, 57, 58,
    62, 63, 64, 66, 69, 80,
    83, 85, 88, 94, 110, 111,
    112
Friendship, 6, 15, 92
Grace, 1, 2, 11, 19, 20, 21,
    22, 23, 24, 25, 27, 28,
    29, 32, 33, 34, 35, 37,
    38, 39, 40, 41, 42, 45,
    46, 47, 48, 49, 50, 51,
    53, 54, 57, 58, 59, 60,

Subject Index

61, 62, 63, 64, 66, 69, 73, 77, 78, 80, 83, 85, 86, 88, 94, 104, 105, 110, 111, 112
Gregory of Nazianzus, 18
Hannibal, 80
Hell, 49, 50
Heresy, 27, 76, 77, 79, 85, 87, 89, 98, 100, 104, 107, 110
Hilary of Poitiers, 73
Holy Spirit, 34, 45, 46, 49, 63, 65
Hospitality, 85, 101, 107
Human merit, 23, 33, 50, 51, 66, 72
Human merits, 37, 38, 41, 44, 47, 58, 59, 60, 61, 62, 80
Human nature, 23, 63, 72
Ignatius of Antioch, 18
Infant baptism, 65
Innocent I, 74, 86
Jerome, 70, 73
John Chrysostom, 73
Julian, 71, 74, 76, 105, 118
Justification, 59
Justinian, 81
Lactantius, 73

Law of God, 28, 48, 55, 56, 57, 63
Manichaeans, 43
Manichaeism, 72, 93, 100
Monnica, 90, 93, 105
Nebridius, 92
Neoplatonism, 93
Nestorius of Constantinople, 75
Obedience, 56, 64
Original sin, 49
Pachomius, 96
Paedobaptism, 48
Pastoral theology, 1, 13, 24, 90, 95, 109
Patricius, 90
Paul Orosius, 101
Pelagianism, 1, 2, 10, 13, 20, 21, 22, 23, 27, 37, 38, 41, 44, 50, 53, 54, 55, 56, 58, 60, 63, 64, 66, 69, 70, 71, 72, 73, 74, 75, 76, 77, 78, 81, 82, 85, 86, 87, 89, 98, 106, 107, 110, 111, 113, 120, 121
Pelagius, 22, 41, 69, 70, 71, 72, 73, 78, 82, 105, 115, 116, 120

God Crowns His Own Gifts

Perfectionism, 70
Persecution, 18
Philosophy, 13, 92
Polycarp of Smyrna, 18
Possidius, 95, 98, 99, 119
Prayer, 45, 57, 64
Predestination, 29, 31, 32, 106
Profuturus, 102
Protestant theology, 17
Quintianus, 102
Reformation, 17, 19, 46, 116
Regeneration, 49
Roman Catholicism, 17, 75
Sabinus, 84
Scipio, 81, 116
Second Punic War, 81
Semi-Pelagian, 21
Simplician, 28, 44, 94
Sixtus, 22, 23, 37, 75, 76, 77, 78, 79, 85, 87, 101, 106, 110, 111, 114, 118
Soteriology, 30, 109
Thrashers, 92
Trajan, 81
Valentinus, 54, 83, 84, 85, 93, 101, 106, 108
Valerius of Hippo, 94
Xystus the Martyr, 73
Zosimus, 74, 76, 86

Scripture Index

Old Testament

Psalms
    62:13 48
Proverbs
    1:8 42
    3:39 42
    8:35— 25
    19:3 42

Isaiah
    11:2–3 29
Ezekiel
    18:31–32 50
    36:26 50
Zechariah
    1:3 44

New Testament

Matthew
    6:19 42
    11:28 xiv
    16:27 48
    26:41 43
John
    1:14 xiv
    1:16 48
    15:5 47
Romans
    2:6 48
    2:12 42
    3:20— 49
    4:5 50
    6:23 33
    7:7–13 49
    9:18–20 28
    9:20 34
1 Corinthians
    4:7 .... 29, 30, 46
    15:9 44
    15:10 44
    15:34 42

Scripture Index

Galatians
   2:16 49
Ephesians
   1:4 18
   2:8–9 47
   2:10 47
Philippians
   2:6–11 xiv

1 Timothy
   3:2 95
2 Timothy
   1:7 51
   4:6–8 45
James
   1:13–15 42

www.ingramcontent.com/pod-product-compliance
Lightning Source LLC
Chambersburg PA
CBHW070917080526
44589CB00013B/1329